What SUCCESSFUL
Teachers Do in
Diverse Classrooms

What SUCCESSFUL Teachers Do in Diverse Classrooms

 71 Research-Based Classroom Strategies for New and Veteran Teachers

Neal A. Glasgow ● Sarah J. McNary ● Cathy D. Hicks

CORWIN PRESS
A Sage Publications Company
Thousand Oaks, California

For information:

Corwin Press
A Sage Publications Company
2455 Teller Road
Thousand Oaks, California 91320
www.corwinpress.com

Sage Publications Ltd.
1 Oliver's Yard
55 City Road
London EC1Y 1SP
United Kingdom

Sage Publications India Pvt. Ltd.
B-42, Panchsheel Enclave
Post Box 4109
New Delhi 110 017 India

Printed in the United States of America

Library of Congress Cataloging-in-Publication Data

Glasgow, Neal A.
What successful teachers do in diverse classrooms: 71 research-based classroom strategies for new and veteran teachers / by Neal A. Glasgow, Sarah J. McNary, and Cathy D. Hicks.
        p. cm.
Includes bibliographical references and index.
ISBN 1-4129-1616-X (cloth)
ISBN 1-4129-1617-8 (pbk.)
    1. Teaching—United States. 2. Multicultural education—United States. I. McNary, Sarah J., 1967- II. Hicks, Cathy D. III. Title.
LB1025.3.G517 2006
371.102—dc22

                                                        2005036543

This book is printed on acid-free paper.

06 07 08 09 10   9 8 7 6 5 4 3 2 1

Acquisitions Editor:	Faye Zucker
Editorial Assistant:	Gem Rabanera
Production Editor:	Denise Santoyo
Typesetter:	C&M Digitals (P) Ltd.
Indexer:	Rick Hurd
Cover Designer:	Michael Dubowe

Contents

Chapter 2. Including Students With Special Education Needs   31

Chapter 3. Cultivating Gender Sensitivity   65

Foreword

Educational change depends on what teachers think and do—it's as simple and as complex as that.

Michael Fullan

One of the major challenges facing teachers today is how to best meet the needs of diverse learners. With the population of diverse learners in our nation's schools steadily increasing, teachers serious about educational reform are seeking to better understand not only *who* diverse learners are, but also *what* they need to succeed. Although we know teachers want to provide all students with an excellent education, diverse learners often receive a less-than-equitable learning experience. For this reason, the inclusive strategies outlined in this book are timely. To address this growing need, the authors of this book provide a practical "how to" approach to help teachers begin the delicate dialogue of addressing the complex needs of diverse learners. Exploring these research-based strategies clearly involves a conscious decision to move beyond traditional teaching methods toward a more constructivist classroom environment in which the historical sociocultural experiences of all learners create the foundation for collaborative learning.

During the 30 years I have educated diverse learners as a teacher, counselor, and administrator in the San Dieguito Union High School District, and presently at the San Diego County Office of Education, I am continually reminded that the most successful teachers in diverse classrooms seek to better understand themselves, as well as their students. These self-reflective teachers continually examine their sociocultural and linguistic attitudes, rooted in their own personal experiences. The authors of this text provide a solid overview of straightforward strategies, which inevitably lead teachers to reflect more deeply on this multifaceted topic: How can we best assure equity for all students? How can our schools foster a democratic society? How can schools support teacher collaboration and reflection?

Because teachers are lifelong learners, they are continually finding new ways to meet the needs of their diverse learners. From professional development to new certifications, teachers have many options to expand their understanding of all students. The strategies in this book serve as a catalyst for revamping teaching methods and an invitation for new enriching classroom experiences. I support the authors as they embrace an expansive definition of diversity with topics ranging from gender equity to students with special needs. Once teachers begin to explore these strategies, they will clearly see how they fit into a constructivist classroom by fostering collaboration among students, by using multicultural resources, and by reinforcing the use of authentic assessments. By incorporating these strategies into their teaching repertoire, reflective teachers will not only continue to learn about themselves and their students, but they will also transform their classrooms by modeling inclusive behaviors and attitudes. I applaud the authors' commitment to improve the learning environment in the diverse classroom.

—Donna Heath
Senior Director, Learning Resources and Educational Technology
San Diego County Office of Education

Preface

The history of multicultural education in the United States arguably begins with the Civil Rights Movement of the 1950s and 1960s. Numerous definitions of multicultural education have been proposed by scholars, researchers, organizations, and individuals since that time. Constructing the multicultural paradigm is an ever-changing process in response to the politics and pressures of changing times. It is rare that classroom teachers, academics, and special interest groups have the same definition for multicultural education. As with any conversation on education and educational practice, individuals tend to mold ideas and philosophy to fit their particular perspective.

For many, the boundaries of multicultural education center around racial and ethnic categories, yet others espouse a broader view. To other, less visible, groups in the multicultural mix, the racial and ethnic categories seem to drown out the voices that also promote classroom consideration for their specific perspectives. Other specific cultural groups—representing gender, sexual orientation, special education, white ethnic groups, and others—compete for more consideration by educators. Too many voices can be confusing for teachers and add to the complexity of learning environments.

With so many voices calling for consideration, where do caring teachers go for guidance? Where do we as multiculturally inclusive teachers go to find out what works and what doesn't? What's important and what isn't? What works in one specific school setting (like yours) but not in another?

Unlike many other professions, the primary literature featuring educational research, experimentation, and investigation is usually a world away from the day-to-day grind of the classroom teacher. Also, it is rare for the most current information from academic research to filter into the professional life of a classroom teacher.

Yet, this information does exist and forms a body of knowledge that can be used to improve our craft. There is research on how teachers learn to teach most effectively, how students "learn to learn" best, and, yes, how multicultural principles can best fit into schools, classrooms, and curriculum. A simple key word search of the Internet using the phrase "multicultural education" reveals more than 9 million hits in .07 seconds. Adding the word "research" to the phrase yields more than 3 million hits. Yes, there is a wealth of information out there and much of it is supported by scientific data to help define what works and what doesn't. Some of this information can make us all better at what we do in classrooms and help us to improve our understanding of the developing multicultural world.

We know experience is a great teacher, but there are faster, more humane, and more efficient means of teaching and learning about multicultural education for teachers. Coupling the most effective and valid research with experienced teachers and their knowledge of their own communities yields a powerful, effective, rewarding, and highly beneficial learning environment for students.

The purpose of this book is to give a more proactive voice to the research and the researchers who ask and answer the important questions about multiculturalism in educational environments. Filtered through our own experiences in schools, we hope to make the valuable products of this research and inquiry available to all those involved and concerned with the goals of multicultural aims and objectives. Educators don't have to wait for experience to teach them; they can learn from the experiences of others, use what works, and avoid what doesn't. They then can combine what they already know with new knowledge. For those new to the inclusion of multicultural thought into classrooms, our book provides a shortcut to multicultural literacy.

This book is not meant to be read sequentially as one would read a novel. Rather, our objective is to focus on useful and practical educational research that translates into a range of choices and solutions to individual teaching and learning problems typically faced by those practicing the inclusion of multicultural themes. Within the chapters of the book, we present a wide range of multicultural instructional strategies and suggestions based on educational, psychological, and sociological studies. Strategies are presented and structured in a user-friendly format:

Strategy: A simple, concise statement of a classroom or professional development strategy dealing with multiculturalism in an educational setting.

What the Research Says: A brief discussion of the research that led to the strategy. This section should simply give the educator some confidence in, and a deeper understanding of, the principle(s) being discussed as a strategy.

Classroom Applications: A description of how this strategy can be used in the classroom.

Precautions and Possible Pitfalls: Caveats intended to make possible a reasonably flawless implementation of the strategy. We try to help teachers avoid common difficulties before they occur.

Source(s): This is the original journal article, conference proceeding, or book reporting the basic research we used to develop the main points of the strategies, research synthesis, classroom applications, precautions, and professional development applications. Readers who wish to follow up with additional reading and research are urged to do so. Note that not all sources are references cited in the text.

It is our hope that if those new to multiculturalism in the classroom accept some of these strategies, maybe they can avoid the feelings of inadequacy and uneasiness that many of us experience when we first start working with new concepts. Veteran educators can also benefit from the knowledge gained from new or recent research. Given the tremendous need for new multicultural strategies, we cannot afford to let potentially good information and instructional methods slip by.

Depending on the reader's level of experience or location, there may be strategies that presumably don't apply. Also, as in many new endeavors, some teachers may not know what they don't know. We ask that you consider coming back and revisiting this book from time to time to refresh your thinking and seek inspiration for new professional situations you may be faced with. Changing demographics, policies, and instructional emphasis may require a new look at potential solutions to new problems.

Teaching and education in general have never been more exciting or more challenging than they are today. Expectations for teachers, schools, and students continue to rise. The more multicultural resources educators have at their fingertips to assist students along their educational journey, the better the outcome for society. We hope all educators will find this book a useful and highly practical solution to defining and embracing the goals of multicultural education today.

Acknowledgements

We are grateful to the people at Corwin Press, especially Faye Zucker for her collaboration and support.

Sarah McNary is grateful to coauthors Cathy Hicks and Neal Glasgow for their dedication to education based on research. Many thanks also go to the students she has worked with over the past 15 years who have taught her more about diversity and the importance of individualized instruction than any formal education could have.

Loving gratitude goes to her husband, Dave, and her children, Erica and Alex, for their unending support of her writing efforts. Her deepest thanks go to her mother, Margaret, who is the most gracious person she knows. Finally, she would like to acknowledge the tremendous confidence and cheerleading her sisters, Jacqueline and Caroline, have conveyed throughout her life.

Neal Glasgow gratefully acknowledges his parents, Frank and Leota Glasgow, for their humanitarian philosophy during the 1950s and the 1960s. Their quiet, often unspoken, view of the diverse world is still an inspiration and guide. Further, he acknowledges and appreciates his son Christian's insight into sexual orientation and society. Christian works in a world his father wouldn't have known about without the benefit of reflections from and conversations with his son. He would like to thank Ron Hopkins and Rik Frank for their review, reflection, and suggestions contributing to many of the strategies. Finally, he thanks his coauthors, Cathy Hicks and Sarah McNary for their skill and insight into the world of diversity and education and contribution to the important conversation about diversity and the classroom.

Cathy Hicks is thankful to the more than 5,000 students she has worked with in a career spanning three decades. They have taught her much about the richness of a diverse classroom and indeed about life itself. She is grateful to coauthors Sarah McNary and Neal Glasgow for their dedication and expertise in working with students. Her deepest thanks go to her husband, Bob, and her children, Summer and Hunter, for their love and support. She would also like to acknowledge the teachers in the San Dieguito Union High School District who work tirelessly to make a difference in the lives of *all* students. And a final acknowledgement and heartfelt thank you to Victor Villasenor, one of her favorite authors, for telling his story through his many outstanding books.

Corwin Press would like to thank the following reviewers for their contributions to this book:

Thomas S.C. Farrell, Associate Professor, Brock University, St. Catharines, ON, Canada

Elise Geither, Instructor, Baldwin-Wallace College, Ridgeville, OH

Steve Hutton, Educational Consultant, Kentucky Department of Education's Highly Skilled Educator Program, KY

Toby Karten, Graduate Instructor, College of New Jersey and Gratz College, PA.

Verena Shanin, ESOL Teacher, Berea Middle School, Greenville, SC

William Sommers, Teacher, Eden Prairie Public Schools, Eden Prairie, MN

About the Authors

**Neal A. Glasgow** has been involved in education on many levels. His experience includes serving as a secondary school science and art teacher both in California and New York, as a university biotechnology teaching laboratory director and laboratory technician, as an educational consultant, and as a frequent educational speaker on many topics. He is the author or coauthor of seven books on educational topics: *Tips for the Science Teacher: Research-Based Strategies to Help Students Learn* (2001); *New Curriculum for New Times: A Guide to Student-Centered, Problem-Based Learning* (1997); *Doing Science: Innovative Curriculum Beyond the Textbook for the Life Science Classroom* (1997); *Taking the Classroom Into the Community: A Guide Book* (1996); *What Successful Teachers Do: 91 Research-Based Strategies for New and Veteran Teachers* (2003); *What Successful Mentors Do: 81 Research-Based Strategies for New Teacher Induction, Training, and Support* (2004); and *What Successful Teachers Do in Inclusive Classrooms: 60 Research-Based Strategies That Help Special Learners Succeed* (2005). He is currently teaching AP History and art at San Dieguito Academy High School, a California public high school of choice, and continues to conduct research and write on educational topics as well as work on various personal art projects. He is married, is the father of two grown sons, and has one grandson.

**Sarah J. McNary** is currently teaching a credit recovery program for the San Dieguito Union High School District in Southern California, where she is also the district's consultant for special education working with the Beginning Teacher Support and Assessment (BTSA) program. She is also a faculty member in the Masters of Education program for the University of Phoenix. Over the last 15 years she has taught SH, SDC, RSP, and general education classes at the elementary, middle school, and high school levels. She is a frequent presenter on a variety of aspects of inclusive education and meeting

the needs of a diverse student population. She is coauthor of *What Successful Mentors Do: 81 Research-Based Strategies for New Teacher Induction, Training, and Support* (2004) and *What Successful Teachers Do in Inclusive Classrooms: 60 Research-Based Strategies That Help Special Learners Succeed* (2005). She is innately curious and is a firm believer in lifelong learning. When asked why she loves teaching, Sarah answers, "Because there is simply nothing better than making a difference in the life of a child." She and her husband split their time between Encinitas and their mountain home. She is also the mother of two teenagers.

 **Cathy D. Hicks** is currently the Beginning Teacher Support and Assessment (BTSA)/Induction Program Coordinator for the San Dieguito Union High School District in Southern California. She oversees a two-year induction program for new teachers. She is also part of the adjunct faculty at California State University at San Marcos and serves on the Executive Board of the California Association of School Health Educators (CASHE). She has presented at more than a dozen mentor-teacher leader conferences. Cathy has taught at the secondary level for 27 years. She is coauthor of *What Successful Teachers Do: 91 Research-Based Strategies for New and Veteran Teachers* (2003); *What Successful Mentors Do: 81 Research-Based Strategies for New Teacher Induction, Training, and Support* (2004); and *What Successful Teachers Do in Inclusive Classrooms: 60 Research-Based Strategies That Help Special Learners Succeed* (2005). She believes the most effective teachers are the ones who never settle for "good enough" but continue to grow, stretch, reflect, create, collaborate, and take risks throughout their teaching careers. Cathy is married and has two grown children and one adorable granddaughter.

Introduction

Those of us who are involved in effectively teaching a diverse student body need to share what we have learned (often through trial and error). There are a myriad of ways to address the unique issues each student brings to the classroom, and to facilitate learning we must first understand the individual cultural context of each student. It is an ongoing process, and each of the authors of this book has come to answer it in a different way.

Neal Glasgow

One of the wonderful things about teaching Advanced Placement Art History is that the curriculum and assessment are clear and well defined. The course is designed as a college-level survey covering the highlights of the creation and use of art and architecture over the length and breadth of human history. There is very little choice in what content is covered to help students pass the Advanced Placement test. It's clear the "assessment tail wags the curriculum dog" in Advanced Placement Art History. I don't have the option to customize instruction to my specific localized mix of students. I can change how I teach, but not much of what I teach as the tests draw questions from anywhere in the art history world. I am always under pressure to "fit" it all in before the test.

So what makes this an interesting story? Unlike most courses, my "multicultural" responsibility is easy to see. A search of the Advanced Placement Art History Web site finds the exact proportion of how the "multicultural" mandate fits into the curriculum. The course content is divided between Western art, defined as art "within the European tradition," and art "beyond the European artistic tradition." Art classified beyond the European tradition includes art originating in Africa (including Egypt), the Americas (Central and South America and Native American), Asia, Near East, art of Oceania, and the global Islamic tradition. In a survey of college and university courses these non-European art traditions make up roughly 20 percent of the art classes offered. The current Advanced Placement Art History test reflects that 20 percent in its questioning.

The Advanced Placement Art History course features an educational approach in which all students acquire an awareness, acceptance, and appreciation of cultural diversity and recognize the contributions of many cultures via an art history context. Unfortunately, few other courses in schools today can make this claim. The multicultural education genre and its exact role in the classroom remains less than clearly defined. Most educators understand the reasons we need to be multiculturally sensitive but may not know exactly how to do that.

Sarah McNary

I was born and raised in Vancouver, Canada, and had the opportunity to attend school in a time when cultural differences were accentuated and celebrated. Even today, many Canadians define themselves as Chinese Canadian, French Canadian, Russian Canadian, and so forth. Their ethnic heritage precedes their current citizenship, and the common belief is that individuality is to be valued.

When I came to teach in the United States, it was a small step to embrace the cultural differences I found in my students. The real challenge for me came when I began working at a lower-income school a few miles from the Mexican border. Celebrating my students' ethnic culture was easy, but understanding the issues they faced because of their socioeconomic status was not. The following year I became a special educator, and my definition of culture expanded once again. My students had a whole other set of concerns related to their disabilities, in addition to their ethnicities and family income levels.

For years, I worked on learning how best to meet my students' individual needs. I read whatever research I could get my hands on and queried my students and their families. Over the last three years, I have been teaching a credit recovery class and, as a result, my view of culture has expanded again. These days, I have the good fortune to know my students as individuals, and the experience has humbled me. There is no one right answer, no one definition of culture, and no single instructional technique that works every time. But there are a variety of techniques that can make all the difference in the right set of circumstances.

Cathy Hicks

Although my career began in the gymnasium, I spent 18 years as a Health Education teacher working with high school students. Because Health is a graduation requirement in our district, I taught almost every student in the school. I valued and embraced the diversity of the students, who came from a variety of cultural backgrounds, in my classroom. Yet their diversity placed a responsibility on my shoulders to ensure that issues were discussed with sensitivity and compassion. The curriculum for

Health deals with many controversial areas including sex education, hate and violence prevention, drug use and prevention, and disease prevention. Each of these areas requires sensitivity to make sure that each student feels safe and respected.

Let me give you an example. Often in American culture, people are comfortable with general conversations about reproduction. Yet in other cultures, reproduction and sexuality can be taboo subjects even to the point of talking about childbirth. I can remember assigning a homework project where students had to interview their parents about the circumstances surrounding their mothers' pregnancies and subsequent births. Some students returned with childbirth videos while others explained that their mothers were embarrassed and said they would complete the paper for the teacher privately. Still other parents were confused by the scientific language used to describe the human body. This assignment also called for sensitivity with regard to students who were adopted or no longer lived with their mothers.

In the last six years working as the director of our district's Beginning Teacher Support and Assessment/Induction program, I have learned that it is important for each teacher, regardless of the subject he or she teaches, to make every student feel emotionally and physically safe and respected. Health classes offer the unique opportunity to bring some of the issues surrounding culture, ethnicity, sexuality, religion, gender, and other topics out into a positive discussion. But other classes can embrace these differences in a supportive environment. The most important consideration for teachers to remember is that we are teaching students first and the subject matter second.

Making the Multicultural Connection

One day our descendants will think it incredible that we paid so much attention to things like the amount of melanin in our skin or the shape of our eyes or our gender instead of the unique identities of each of us as complex human beings.

Franklin Thomas

 STRATEGY 1: Be sensitive to the diversity of today's classrooms.

What the Research Says

 That today's schools are more diverse than ever is undeniable. According to the Federal Interagency Forum on Child and Family Statistics (1998), one in every three students currently attending primary or secondary schools is of a racial or ethnic minority. It is predicted that students of color will make up almost

50 percent of the U.S. school-age population by 2020 (Banks & Banks, 2001). The children born of the large influx of immigrants to the United States in the last several decades currently comprise approximately 20 percent of the children in America, providing a kaleidoscope of cultural and language differences to many classrooms (Dugger, 1998).

Cultural and language differences are only a part of the diversity in our schools. One in five children under the age of 18 years currently lives below the poverty line. The traditional two-parent family is becoming the minority. Less than half of America's children currently live with both biological parents, with almost 60 percent of all students living in a single-parent household by the time they reach the age of 18 years (Salend, 2001). All of this is occurring at a time when schools are working toward mainstreaming and inclusion of nearly 11 percent of school-age children who are classified as *disabled* (U.S. Department of Education, 1995). Certainly the challenges in today's classrooms have never been greater. Many teacher preparation programs now include classes to help prepare future teachers for cross-cultural, inclusive instruction. Zeichner (1993) proposed that the key characteristics of these programs provide for the dynamics of prejudice and racism.

Classroom Applications

Even in today's society, some classrooms seem to be focusing on the "differences" and difficulties involved in multicultural education, rather than embracing these differences as enriching, desirable, inevitable, natural, and positive forces. Teachers must not only acknowledge the more obvious diversity issues such as color and physical disability, but also be aware of the *cultural* diversity of students and families. In selecting curriculum it is important to see if examples of diversity are represented. Are the visual examples only of whites? Are the holidays represented in literature only those celebrated by Christians? Are the needs and emotions of people with disabilities presented? When having a discussion of families, it is important to stress that not all family units are alike. When sending a note home to parents, it is better to have it addressed to the "parent or guardian of" instead of "mother" or "father."

A teacher once asked her students to describe their bedrooms and draw pictures of them. What this teacher didn't realize was that several students did not have their own bedrooms but shared the room with four or five other siblings. Disclosing this information to the class by reading the story and showing the drawing might be embarrassing for the students. By the same token, all teachers must be especially aware of district and state education codes with regard to celebrating religious holidays in the classroom. What about the student who doesn't celebrate Christian or Jewish holidays? Rather than ask a student to write a story about his or her favorite Christmas memory, the teacher might assign students to write about a favorite family tradition.

One question teachers should ask themselves is, "Could this question, example, or assignment make a student feel uncomfortable with regard to his or her race, religion, ethnicity, or cultural background?" Designing a richly diverse curriculum does not have to be difficult, it simply takes thought and consideration. The use of cooperative learning groups lends itself particularly well to teaching students with differing abilities in the same classroom. Students should be grouped with consideration to differences in gender, race, ethnicity, and ability. Using assignments and activities that incorporate the recognition of multiple intelligences is necessary and particularly effective in responding to student diversity.

Precautions and Possible Pitfalls

It is of the utmost importance that teachers are prepared for cross-cultural, inclusive instruction. Classes in teacher education programs must include information about the characteristics of prejudice and racism, successful examples of teaching ethnic and language minority students, and instruction that provides both social support for students and intellectual challenge.

Teachers must also be sensitive to issues involving money. Perhaps every child in class can't afford the cost of a field trip. For one high school that was considering putting ATM machines on campus, the realization of the ways this could further divide students into "the haves" and "the have nots" caused administrators to rethink their decision.

Teachers should consult with experienced, exemplary teachers or school administrators before meeting with parents of immigrant students to determine if a translator might be needed, or if there is any specific information about that student's family culture that might assist the teacher in having a successful meeting. The same is true for a student with disabilities. The special education teacher and the Individualized Education Program (IEP) can provide beneficial information to the teacher. The more a teacher is sensitive to the richness of the diversity in his or her classroom, the more successful and equitable today's classrooms will become.

Sources

Banks, J. A., & Banks, C. A. M. (2001). *Multicultural education: Issues and perspectives* (4th ed.). New York: John Wiley.

Dugger, C. W. (1998, March 21). Among young of immigrants, outlook rises. *New York Times*, pp. A1, A11.

Federal Interagency Forum on Child and Family Statistics. (1998). *America's children: Key national indicators of well-being.* Washington, DC: U.S. Government Printing Office.

Salend, S. J. (2001). *Creating inclusive classrooms: Effective and reflective practices* (4th ed.). Upper Saddle River, NJ: Merrill Prentice Hall.

U.S. Department of Education. (1995). *17th annual report to Congress on the implementation of IDEA.* Washington, DC: Author.

Zeichner, K. M. (1993). *Educating teachers for diversity.* East Lansing, MI: National Center for Research on Teacher Learning.

STRATEGY 2: *Move beyond "color blind" teaching and take the time to know students in specific localized cultural contexts.*

What the Research Says

 More than 90 percent of classroom teachers in the United States are white, according to the National Education Association in 1997. It is no secret that they are teaching students who are of very different backgrounds from the teachers and from their fellow students. This statistic highlights a huge racial and cultural divide between teachers and the students in their classrooms. The gap is projected to keep growing. The Johnson study (2002) examined how white teachers conceptualized their own race and their students' races, and how these views might affect teachers' professional choices and practices.

This study gathered data through interviews of six white teachers from racially diverse classrooms who had been "nominated" as being aware of race and racism by a panel of experts. The teachers' responses to semi-structured interviews focused on their racial identity along with a classroom visit and observations of teacher-student interactions. Johnson's analysis (Johnson, 2002) revealed that teachers' cognition of racial and ethnic awareness was affected by the following:

- A perceived identity as "outsiders" due to social class background or sexual orientation that allowed them to "dis-identify" with the white mainstream
- Living and working with individuals of other races in relationships that approximated "equal status," which exposed them to "insider" views on race and racism
- Personal religious or philosophical beliefs that emphasized equality and social justice concerns (p. 153)

The information presented suggested implications for restructuring teacher education programs that included the following (Johnson, 2002, p. 153):

- Revising candidate selection criteria
- Increasing the racial diversity of students and faculty
- Experiencing some type of immersion program in communities of color
- Using autobiographical narratives, which serve as starting points for reflection and as pedagogical devices for identifying related issues

Classroom Applications

From the perspective of the white teacher, the term *color blind* is often used to describe a teacher's idealized view on race and ethnic background. Many believe it is wrong to notice or speak about the race of their students. A teacher observed in the Johnson study stated she used to think it was wrong to notice the race of her students but she had changed her view. She said, "Before I had that liberal mentality, that mentality where everyone is the same. Well, that's not true. This person's experience may be very different than mine and I need to understand that before teaching them or before engaging them in conversation" (Johnson, 2002, p. 161).

It is not race so much as it is the cultural context that a teacher needs to understand to better serve his or her students. For an educator, it is class background, sexual orientation, and racial and ethnic affiliations that must be understood. This moves the teacher beyond the "Black-White paradigm." This Black-White paradigm *racializes* African Americans but not whites. Teachers fail to see culture in their African American students and the huge range of ethnic diversity within their population.

Beyond the Black-White paradigm, the background of Hispanics and Hispanic social grouping is very different and exists well beyond the more known and understood Black-White paradigm. There is no legacy of slavery, and skin color is not as often seen as a clear racial distinction. Hispanics are discriminated against less for skin color but more for their Hispanic cultural stereotypes, surnames, language, and other characteristics that are more likely targets for bias.

In a hypothetical community, economically disadvantaged whites may culturally identify more closely with other economically disadvantaged racial minorities than with white middle-class values. The "white privilege" of the educated white teacher is far from their lives. Cultural differences can fall more along economic and educational background lines than skin color or other more familiar ethnic factors. Because of this, in some cases, it is the economic and educational divide that separates a teacher's cultural context from his or her student's context, not ethnic or racial. When a teacher looks out into the classroom into that sea of faces, skin color only scratches the surface of the differences between individual students and between the students and the teacher.

Precautions and Potential Pitfalls

In the study of logic lies the fallacy of oversimplification. Some will try to, in an effort to understand, oversimplify a very complex social issue. There are so many variables in any community that overlaying a cliché understanding over any community would be a mistake. An accurate cultural context is built over time as a teacher becomes familiar with a community and the school's demographics. Moving beyond the color-blind approach means that a teacher becomes truly engaged in seeking a clear understanding of a community and a student's place in it.

Sources

Johnson, L. (2002). "My eyes have been opened": White teachers and racial awareness. *Journal of Teacher Education, 53*(2), 153–167.

National Education Association. (1997). *Status of the American public school teacher, 1995–96.* Washington, DC: Author.

STRATEGY 3: *Reflect on how multicultural competence is defined today.*

What the Research Says

Stuart (2004) reviews the history of the multicultural genre within the discipline of clinical psychology and the evolution of how multicultural competencies and perspectives have changed over the years. Current research (American Psychological Association, 2002) finds a central premise that states, "psychologists should be aware of and respect cultural, individual and role differences . . . must practice only within the boundaries of their competence . . . and must make a reasonable effort to obtain research, training, consultation, or study." Stuart outlines the history of multiculturalism and its development as a major factor in clinical psychology. Finally, Stuart provides and describes practical suggestions for those interested in refining their approach to understanding how ethnicity and culture influence a person's life perspective.

Stuart (2004) states that people tend to believe that others see the world the same way. Further, he states that when people do acknowledge different perspectives, they normally form convenient notions about the differences that create little more than the illusion of understanding. For the psychological community, Stuart goes on to say that to achieve true multicultural understanding, psychologists need to learn how to find and use resources that allow them, "to approach clients with sensitivity to their diversity while avoiding the trap of pan-ethnic labels . . . which dilute and obscure the moderating effects of national origin, immigration history, religion and tradition," not to mention individual differences within larger groups.

Stuart notes that more than 1 in 10 Americans are foreign born and 1 in 3 belong to groups identified as minorities. The majority of these live in three states: California, Hawaii, and New Mexico. Whereas the term *culture* was first used in the late 19th and early 20th centuries, the term *multicultural* did not appear in the *Oxford English Dictionary* until 1989.

Classroom Applications

In education, multicultural competence can be defined as the ability of the teacher to understand and constructively relate to the uniqueness of each student in light of the diverse cultures that influence each student's identity and perspective. Taken further, parents of students and the communities that feed into a teacher's classroom must also be considered. To achieve this level of competence, it is necessary to avoid stereotypes and simple cliché characterizations and to identify the multicultural influences that can help define appropriate discourse, curriculum, and instructional strategies. Specifically, teachers need to make the effort to discover who their specific students are in an effort to better meet their diverse needs.

Teachers should develop their skills at discovering each student's cultural outlook. Students do not always see multiculturalism in the same way as the teacher. Teachers can develop the skills it takes to see how their students explain and justify their lives and how their perspectives define what they think to be their true selves. Good teaching involves both acceptance and change. Change is more meaningful and easier to accomplish when it is grounded in acceptance and understanding of the student's own reality.

Teachers need to model the same reflective techniques they want their students to exhibit. Multicultural sensitivity begins very personally in the minds of teachers. When a teacher's biases go unchecked, some of a teacher's beliefs can turn into predictions and self-fulfilling prophecies about the behavior of a student or a student group. Simple sharing activities, journaling, or oral presentations can help students communicate their ideas. These activities can also help establish a positive classroom community.

Teachers should tread lightly and wait for "teachable moments." There are times where there are prominent differences, but it is very important to remember there are many other group behaviors and beliefs that are common across cultures. The observation of a few differences doesn't necessarily indicate that everything else in the culture is different too. Resist overgeneralizing from one or two differences, which can lead to stereotyping.

Teachers need to model for their students an ability to resist coming to conclusions with limited data. Because of the complexity of culture or cultures, knowledge and information from literature often suffers from flawed collection techniques. Small sample sizes or too many variables can lead researchers to inaccurate conclusions. Ideas should be looked at with a critical eye.

Teachers also need to encourage critical thinking in their students during discussions about multiculturalism as it is a complex issue. People have far more diversity than is reflected in language categories. Spanish speakers of the U.S. Southwest, for example, comprise a large range of cultures, backgrounds, socioeconomic status, and ethnic origins. There is a high degree of bias and stereotyping that occurs within this group that shares the same language. Many ethnic groups vary depending on which generation they happen to be from and how removed they are from their country of origin. Native Americans vary greatly in where they are culturally and in their worldviews. It is better to describe rather than categorize a student's or group's identity or behavior.

Teachers can help students understand individuality by learning about each student's acceptance of peer-group and cultural beliefs. Although it may seem that certain students express identification with a particular ethnic or cultural group, they do not always reveal which specific beliefs or practices they really accept, how strongly they express those beliefs, and whether they reject certain ideas outright. Getting to know the individual student well and developing an accepting and trusting relationship can help create understanding.

Teachers need to be aware of their students' ethnic and worldviews when selecting discussion topics. For example, all African American students have not universally embraced multicultural programs that emphasize African and African American history and culture. Some students state they feel little or no affinity for the contents of these programs. Their connections are to the United States and, more important, to their own local communities and personal histories. They state they are more concerned with the reality of their current situations rather than searching for connections to the past. There are individual or family philosophical conflicts between historical context, relevancy, importance, and validity. In these situations, curricular content can be seen as a "force fit." Keep in mind that a teacher's enthusiasm for a particular classroom instructional style may not always be shared by students.

Teachers need to be aware of and sensitive to alternative beliefs and perspectives. Sensitivity to a student's personal culture is to understand the unique and personal way in which values, beliefs, and practices help create identity and meaning. A lack of sensitivity, empathy, and respect limits the rapport a teacher needs to be effective. For example, various cultures have different views on the value of education. In some cultures, there is a double standard and expectation for boys and girls within the same family or community. Many times teachers see the potential of female students but also see the conflict these students have with their families' expectations. Teachers have an obligation to offer the alternative views necessary to facilitate a student's growth. In instances such as these, knowledge of the belief systems shared by the family and student helps.

Ultimately, multicultural competence requires self-reflection, critical skills in evaluating curriculum and other materials, thoughtful accumulation of personal teaching wisdom, and great sensitivity to the uniqueness of each class and each student.

Precautions and Potential Pitfalls

 Teachers need to realize that these approaches take time to adopt within a personal style. Teaching styles develop over time and through experience. Teachers can develop their style by "trying on" new behaviors and seeing which ones "fit" or work in certain settings.

Don't forget to solicit students for their suggestions on how to best address the issues of multiculturalism in the classroom. Often they are a positive source of instructional ideas, and using their suggestions increases their ownership in the classroom community.

Sources

American Psychological Association. (2002). Ethical principles and code of conduct. *American Psychologist, 57,* 1060–1073.

Stuart, R. B. (2004). Twelve practical suggestions for achieving multicultural competence. *Professional Psychology: Research and Practice, 35*(1), 3–9.

 STRATEGY 4: Help immigrant students by understanding their personal beliefs.

What the Research Says

 Researchers Exposito and Favela (2003) examined the issues surrounding immigrant students and their teachers. They identified five themes that are found in highly effective teachers:

1. *Ideological clarity*: Teachers need to take the time to evaluate their own personal beliefs about a given culture. Often these ideas are developed in the teacher's own childhood experiences and may extend to ideas about how people should live and what they should be trying to achieve.

2. *Ideology based on middle-class values*: Teachers also need to evaluate their beliefs and attitudes about how families should function if that view is based on a standard middle-class white family structure. Efforts should be made to understand the immigrant family structure and its process.

3. *Ideological baggage*: Teachers need to examine their own educational experiences. Journaling can be an effective way to uncover these issues. Some teachers have had negative experiences, which can motivate them to become the positive teachers they wish they'd had.

4. *Asset-based education*: Teachers need to develop a positive outlook regarding the available skills that immigrant families and students can offer. Teachers need to incorporate these "cultural resources" into their classroom instruction.

5. *It only takes one person*: Teachers need to remember that one person can make the difference in helping immigrant students feel comfortable and safe exploring the new while maintaining their own individual cultural traditions.

Classroom Applications

The first step for any teacher who plans to be effective working with immigrant students is to closely examine his or her own personal beliefs. Journaling is often an excellent way to uncover an individual's personal educational experiences. By reviewing one's own educational experiences, a person can examine beliefs held about other cultures; a teacher can understand his or her own feelings about the culture of a particular student who comes from a different background. Taking the time to learn about that culture and finding the positive educational assets that culture can bring to the classroom is the next step. From this point, ongoing critical reflection will facilitate the reciprocal development of both the teacher and the immigrant students. Teachers must ask themselves if their underlying beliefs are helping or hindering their students. They must then make whatever changes are required.

Teachers need to create positive classroom environments that welcome and encourage children of different cultures and experiences to feel valued and respected. By listening to their students and making the extra effort to learn about them as individuals, teachers can help bridge the gap between feeling isolated and lost and feeling secure. Honoring and valuing differences in language and culture sets a positive tone for all students in a classroom.

Precautions and Possible Pitfalls

Some teachers feel that they have nothing to offer students from different cultures if they have never experienced other cultures or learned a second language personally. This is not necessarily the case. By modeling openness and acceptance and taking the time to listen and learn from their students and their families, all teachers can succeed in creating a positive classroom environment for their immigrant students.

Source

Exposito, S., & Favela, A. (2003). Reflective voices: Valuing immigrant students and teaching with ideological clarity. *Urban Review, 35*(1), 73–92.

STRATEGY 5: Make sure white ethnic students get multicultural education too.

What the Research Says

Immigration has been a part of the American experience since the beginning of the country. U.S. history tells us the Great Migration (1885–1925) brought waves of immigrants from both southern and eastern Europe to the United States. For years, the term *melting pot* captured the basic philosophical nature of assimilation into mainstream America as immigrants sacrificed many of their cultural ways to become part of their new country. However, these white immigrants and their second-, third-, and fourth-generation children, while participating fully in being American, often returned to ethnic neighborhoods where the traditions, languages, and customs of their countries of origin persist.

In 1977, Stein and Hill marked the beginning of the white ethnic movement, arguing that the melting pot idea did not work and the descendants of the Great Migration were "unmeltable." Concurrent with this redefinition, the multicultural education movement emerged with the goals of creating educational environments in which students from all cultural groups (gender, sexual orientation, special needs, linguistic, religious, ethnic/racial) would experience educational equality. In contrast to the melting pot idea, the "salad bowl" philosophy replaced the idea of full assimilation. The term *salad bowl* described a concept in which separate and distinct items exist together but are not part of each other. So a person's identity included an ethnic background in addition to being an American. This identity might also include religious background, sexual orientation, and other outward signs of one's heritage or current beliefs.

In 1978, Banks and Gay described the goals of multiethnic education as modifying the total school environment so that it is reflective of the ethnic diversity within American society. The main goals were to help reduce discrimination against ethnic groups, to provide all students with equal educational opportunities, and to help reduce ethnic isolation and encapsulation.

The goal of Wenze's 2004 study was to replicate his previous 1984 study in a public school in Scranton, Pennsylvania. This new study was prompted by a 2000 census indicating a growing cultural diversity in populations entering the Scranton area yet still showing strong evidence of white ethnic grouping. Both studies tried to determine white ethnic children's need for multiethnic education as it was envisioned by their parents. Indicators of ethnic heritage in the Wenze study included frequent ethnic meals, interest in ethnic literature, observance of ethnic customs, feeling closer to family and ethnic members, ethnic customs at weddings, ethnic names in families, membership in ethnic clubs, ethnic language in the home, preferring family members as close friends, subscription to an ethnic newspaper, and embracing ethnic identity along with being an "American."

The objectives of the new study were to determine if ethnic consciousness exists among the parents and whether the locus of ethnicity is in the school or elsewhere. The investigation showed that the center of ethnicity for all survey populations was predominately in the home. However, parents showed an interest in their children learning about ethnic heritage in schools. They also wanted their children to learn about other cultures. In questionnaires, parents saw the school as a place with the potential to teach ethnic heritages. Asked whether parents thought it was a good idea to have ethnically relevant materials in schools, one parent was quoted as saying, "We believe strongly in introducing our children to as many ethnic groups and their traditions as possible. Having the school do the same would lessen the differences."

The Wenze study went on to describe how white ethnicity is defined. Although the original study described multicultural education as programs for ethnic groups who were phenotypically different from the dominant white group, Wenze suggests that white ethnics are another group whose children would benefit from multicultural or multiethnic education. Dense populations of Italian, Polish, Slovak, and Irish groups in neighborhoods next to schools, in addition to churches founded by white ethnic groups, create ethnic consciousness.

Classroom Applications

Twenty-first century classrooms are filled with students of diversity. It's a time when teachers are challenged to provide a form of education that meets the needs of a wide range of ethnicities. To add to the mix, teachers are expected to be sensitive to other inclusive target categories such as gender, sexual orientation, gifted and talented, and special learners. This research adds another inclusive category to the agenda.

The term *white* covers a wide demographic. white ethnicities are often generations removed from their original immigrant ancestors, and the need for multicultural and multiethnic education may not be as clearly defined as it was at the turn of the century. white privilege and entitlement can be a common misconception if all whites are considered to be in the same ethnic genre. The voices of other inclusive or minority groups are loud. Yet, teachers are encouraged to remember that there are many diverse individuals found among white ethnic students as well as among other minority student groups of color and linguistic differences. Many of these groups also share an early history of discrimination and bias.

The results of Wenze's research suggest that there is a desire for culturally relevant curriculum and instruction to enhance the educational opportunities for white ethnic children. All children benefit from learning about their own and other cultures. Some teachers find projects like "I" searches, family trees, and family traditions can provide a good starting point for positive discussions.

Precautions and Potential Pitfalls

Inclusive or minority education, particularly the multicultural variety, is politically loaded with pitfalls. There are many voices competing for a role in defining priorities for reform and restructuring. Many minority or under-represented groups want a voice in how inclusive education is to be identified, created, organized, and implemented. It is very difficult to be politically, ethnically, and morally correct in every situation.

Sources

Banks, J. A., & Gay, G. (1978). Ethnicity in contemporary American society: Toward development of a typology. *Ethnicity, 5,* 238–251.

Stein, H. F., & Hill, R. F. (1977). *The ethnic imperative.* University Park, PA: Pennsylvania State University Press.

Wenze, G. T. (2004). Multiethnic education for white ethnic children: A study revisited. *Multicultural Education, 12*(2), 29–33.

STRATEGY 6: *Cultivate multicultural connections.*

What the Research Says

Making connections when learning mathematics is one of the underlying themes of the National Council of Teachers of Mathematics (NCTM)'s 2005 *Curriculum and Evaluation Standards*. Students should be able to connect what they learn in mathematics with problems that arise in different subjects and with multicultural aspects of our society. Five dimensions of multicultural education have been identified as comprising a framework for mathematics:

1. *Integrate content* to reflect diversity when teaching key concepts.

2. *Construct knowledge* so students understand how people's points of view within a discipline influence the conclusions they reach in a discipline.

3. *Reduce prejudice* so students develop positive attitudes toward different groups of people.

4. *Use instructional techniques* that will promote achievement from diverse groups of students.

5. *Modify the school culture* to ensure that people from diverse groups are empowered and have educational equality.

Classroom Applications

Teachers should take into consideration that disciplines and content areas are not free of cultural influences, that some textbooks have racial biases, and that the history of any discipline should not just be viewed from a Eurocentric perspective (Pugh, 1990). The five principles are not limited to a math curriculum; they can be applied to any discipline. For example:

1. *Integrate content* so that the history of the discipline's content knowledge comes from many cultures and ethnicities. For example, teach students about George Washington Carver, an African American who made major contributions that influenced botany, agribusiness, and biotechnology.

2. *Construct knowledge* so students see the universal nature of the components, concepts, and processes of the discipline and how other cultures and ethnic backgrounds might view them.

3. *Reduce prejudice* by using teaching and learning to eliminate stereotypes. For example, balance the contributions of whites with other ethnic backgrounds and cultures.

4. *Use instructional techniques* that motivate students and demonstrate mutual respect for culture. For example, group together students from diverse cultures for cooperative learning activities; encourage all students to participate in extracurricular activities; and have high expectations for success from all students, regardless of cultural backgrounds.

5. *Modify the school culture.* Make special efforts to work with minority parents, especially parents who are not native English speakers.

Precautions and Possible Pitfalls

 The teacher needs to make sure that multicultural aspects of lessons are not performed in a patronizing manner. Also, a teacher should try to be broad in his or her multicultural focus so that no particular cultural group (e.g., African American, Hispanic, Asian) is excluded. Teachers need to remain cognizant that individual cultural experiences create a filter through which the world is viewed. Recognizing that filter is an important part of self-reflection.

Sources

Banks, J. A. (1994). Transforming the mainstream curriculum. *Educational Leadership, 51*(8), 4–8.

Bishop, A. (1988). Mathematics education in its cultural context. *Educational Studies in Mathematics, 19,* 179–191.

Gallard, A. J. (1992). Creating a multicultural learning environment in science classrooms. *Research Matters—To the Science Teacher,* 1–6.

Moses, R., Kamii, M., Swap, S., & Howard, J. (1989). The algebra project: Organizing in the spirit of Ella. *Harvard Educational Review, 59*(4), 423–443.

Mendez, P. (1989). *The black snowman.* New York: Scholastic.

National Council of Teachers of Mathematics. (2005). *Curriculum and Evaluation Standards.* Reston, VA: Author.

Pugh, S. (1990). Introducing multicultural science teaching to a secondary school. *Secondary Science Review, 71*(256), 131–135.

Strutchens, M. (1995). *Multicultural mathematics: A more inclusive mathematics.* ERIC Digest. Clearinghouse for Science, Mathematics and Environmental Education, Columbus, Ohio. (ERIC Document Reproduction Service No. ED380295)

STRATEGY 7: *Develop and promote a positive ethnic identity.*

What the Research Says

Multicultural contemporary classrooms now trigger issues such as the construction of racial and ethnic identities, gender roles, and socioeconomic status. Within this mix falls a teacher's sense of ethnic identity. Teachers must be aware of the ways in which language, culture, and ethnicity mediate the social constructs of identity. How teachers perceive and interact with these constructs can affect the expectations they have for the students. In this study, Hispanic teachers and Hispanic students were the focus. In comparing white, black, and Chicano self-conceptions, Hurtsfield (1978) concluded that ethnic membership and status often determine an individual's self-description. Minority subjects were more likely than majority subjects to be conscious of racial or ethnic identity. The research cited past studies that found connections between minority teachers who interpreted their own cultural identity and how it played a critical role in their identity as educators. They also noted correlations between self-concept, teacher efficacy, and empowerment.

Ethnic identity can often reflect how individuals recognize the social-political context in which they live. Analysis revealed that for minorities, ethnic self-identification is an individual conceptualization. It is reflected in the heterogeneity found within groups, and ethnic labels are not always interchangeable. Second, it was important that individuals identify themselves individually as too often they are stereotypically lumped together. Third, patterns within groups can be revealing. These three categories of data can be used to increase understanding of distinctiveness within minority groups. For example, some native-born individuals identified themselves as Mexican even though they were not foreign born.

The study produced a variety of recommendations geared toward teacher education programs recognizing the need for minority teachers to work with the questions regarding their teacher and ethnic identities. Above all, education programs need to address and value the cultural knowledge that minority teachers bring with them. They also need to recognize that their identity as educators will affect many areas of their interaction with students.

Classroom Applications

Because today's classrooms, more than ever, are cross-cultural situations, successful teaching depends on positive teacher self-esteem. Ultimately, the way the school and its teachers respond to and support difference affects the degree of school success for many ethnic minority and language minority students.

If a teacher is from a minority culture, how he or she identifies with his or her culture or is seen culturally by the students affects the teaching and learning environment. The research did identify a very heterogeneous mix of cultural self-concepts even within small ethnic groups. Not everyone wants his or her ethnic or cultural background to be subject for reflection or public attention. Individuals have to decide for themselves how their ethnic identity or cultural background becomes or doesn't become an element in their professional lives. Teachers should consider talking to trusted colleagues about the issues or seeking out additional academic research on the topic. There are no easy answers; the individualistic nature of self-ethnic identification doesn't foster *one-size-fits-all* solutions and strategies.

Ultimately, some will see their calling as role models or advocates for their ethnic or cultural background. Others will take the path of assimilation and not want their ethnic and cultural background to be an element in their teaching. Just becoming aware of the choices is a start.

Precautions and Possible Pitfalls

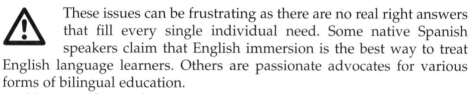 These issues can be frustrating as there are no real right answers that fill every single individual need. Some native Spanish speakers claim that English immersion is the best way to treat English language learners. Others are passionate advocates for various forms of bilingual education.

Many teachers who were language minority students themselves may be tempted to feel that the path personally taken toward success in school is the best one. Teachers' expectations for their students can be biased by their own experiences. Teachers have options to consider in how they perceive themselves, the identities they want to project, and how all of that fits into their own teaching and professional relationships.

Sources

Clark, E. R., & Flores, B. B. (2001). Who am I? The social construction of ethnic identity and the self-perceptions in Latino preservice teachers. *The Urban Review, 33*(2), 69–86.

Clark, E. R., Nystrom, N., & Perez, B. (1996). Language and culture: Critical components of multicultural teacher education. *The Urban Review,* 185–197.

Hurtsfield, J. (1978). Internal colonialism: white, black, and Chicano self-conceptions. *Ethnic and Racial Studies, 1,* 6–79.

STRATEGY 8: Watch for factors of exclusion that influence multicultural curriculum choices.

What the Research Says

Agee's case study (2004) follows the experiences of a young African American English teacher over a 3-year period that encompassed her late preservice coursework, student teaching, and her first years teaching under contract. The subject was a 21-year-old English major. She was one of only two African American students in her English education program. Her teaching experience took place in two high schools. The first was a primarily white school both within the student body and faculty. The second setting was a more diverse experience. This teacher especially wanted to work with disadvantaged students to bring their individual voices and interests into the class mix. The questions Agee was trying to answer included:

- What perspectives does a preservice teacher have on the reading and the teaching of literature?
- How is the young subject of the research, an African American female teacher, able to develop her identity teaching in a suburban high school?
- How do national and state policies, which shape standards and assessment, influence teacher identity formation, especially for teachers who want to use more diverse texts and approaches?
- Are teacher education programs unintentionally maintaining a white, Euro-American hegemony with discourse that makes teachers of color and their perspectives on curriculum invisible?

In her university experience, the subject was highly motivated and encouraged in her classes. She expressed a personal desire to teach multicultural literature using a constructivist style. The goal was to build and use the curriculum, the literature, and a diverse student body's personal experiences to broaden the students' understanding of racial, ethnic, and cultural differences.

Yet, in both her preservice teaching and her first 2 years of contract teaching she found it difficult to implement her goals. Her goals, efforts, and identity as a teacher who would help students explore, begin to understand, and celebrate diversity began to degenerate as she struggled with school policies, mandated assessment preparation, and racial bias. Her disenchantment grew as her imagined identity collided with state mandates, the mainstream construction of a teacher's role, and heavily institutionalized versions and ideologies of curriculum and assessment. According to Agee, "Her story speaks to the gap between progressive teacher education programs and the demands of mandated, high stakes tests on schools and teachers." One result Agee found within the study was the tendency to silence diverse points of view, "a factor that may further contribute to the lack of teachers of color in American schools."

This teacher's story documents how many teachers are not prepared for the constraints on teaching and learning that accompany testing agendas and the personal ethical decisions they will need to make.

Agee described the subject of the study as wanting to be a "change maker" but found there were costs. In the end, the subject found no comfortable zone to realize her dream or remove the intense institutional pressure to comply with mainstream or dominant ideologies.

Agee's research is an example of how many new teachers evolve through their first few years. Agee's research observes and describes many of the experiences that many, if not all, new teachers experience. However, in Agee's view there are a number of more hidden topics of race and power mixed in. Many education majors come into teaching with their personal agendas and are not prepared for the politics and power struggles of teaching and the classroom.

The subject teacher's choice of literature spawned classroom discourse leading to the embarrassment of some students and resistance by others. Discussion brought up racial tensions, and she had little guidance on how to handle racial and ethnic bias within classroom curricular discussions. Other teachers, parents, and students frequently critique literature choices by teachers for validity. Beginning teachers may not have the political capital to fight criticism.

It is also clear that all educational stakeholders (parents, students, community members, etc.) have their own ideas of what teaching and learning is or should be. If students or parents feel threatened by what goes on in the classroom (i.e., grades, not being prepared for testing or college), they will react; teachers who haven't helped the stakeholders prepare for curricular changes risk a backlash.

In the Agee study, while the teacher seemed supported at times in her efforts to work in multicultural curricular goals, there were counterpressures. Discussions within the English department suggested an effort to standardize the curriculum and begin grade-level testing to better prepare students for the state's graduation tests. They wanted curricular unity so instruction didn't overlap. The proposed curriculum, the grade-level tests, and the state graduation tests would all force her to alter her personal plans and limit her personal goals. Being different usually draws attention to the teacher, and, again, new teachers rarely have the power to deviate too far from the mainstream.

In a second setting, the subject's efforts were stymied by the grade-level testing designed to better prepare students for the state tests. She talked about how mandated tests pushed her to teach literature differently than she had planned. She decided to go along with the consensus of the English department, but was very troubled by the power of the testing agenda and the politics of curricular development.

In the beginning of this 3-year study, Agee described a motivated teacher with an interest in developing multicultural educational environments using constructivist approaches with at-risk students. Once she started teaching, she was routinely experiencing dilemmas. How could she balance her early goals and what she hoped to achieve with "the realities of school," which meant trading her early idealism for test scores? She found she had no help in facilitating test preparation or preparing her students to understand other races and cultures through education. By the end of her second contract year she had found no time to add multicultural literature to the traditional required readings. She moved from a constructivist and student-centered approach to a largely teacher-centered approach. The 3-year transition seemed to bring an end to her initial vision of herself as a teacher and her new perspectives regarding curriculum and instruction.

Classroom Applications

It is no secret that there are huge challenges for new teachers between the idealism and expectations of preservice experiences and the realities of teaching actual students in actual school environments. In the case of Agee's research, it was suggested the word *reality* was used as a code word for "white mainstream ideologies" in schools.

New teachers routinely *hit the wall* of classroom reality when transitioning from life as an education student to life as a teacher and educational practitioner. These early rough transition periods are widely believed to be the cause of the high attrition rate for new teachers, particularly new teachers in urban settings.

New teachers need to be made aware of the politics of schools as a workplace. Workplace savvy can help new teachers through discouraging times. One way to begin is to look at curricular development from a new perspective. Rather than dropping all hope of making a difference, new teachers need to think about making "surgical strikes" into existing mandated curriculum. Many times it's the perspective that is taken or the way students view a concept that can make a difference. For example, the battle of the Alamo could be taught from both perspectives, the U.S. side and the Mexican side. By discussing alternative perspectives, teaching is student-centered and builds critical thinking. Students are not told what to think but are only asked to think. In this way, teachers begin to expose biases, stereotypes, inaccuracies, and marginalization in curricular content, pedagogy, and academic policies.

To further examine the issues presented in Agee's work, a different perspective in multicultural or inclusive instructional practices can help. Gorski (2004) said that multicultural or inclusive practices can be defined in two ways. They are summarized here.

Inclusion refers to the extent to which different voices and perspectives are heard in the classroom. There are two levels of inclusion. When most teachers talk about inclusion, they are referring to representational inclusion, or the inclusion of sources or information that closely match or represent the diversity within a particular classroom. For example, if there is a Mexican student in a class, a teacher must be sure to include sources by Mexican authors in the classroom. The second level of inclusion is student-centered inclusion, or the inclusion of the voices and perspectives of the students themselves in the educational experience. Students are the most underused educational resource in most classrooms. A multicultural curriculum encourages them to provide personal multicultural context and perspectives on all subjects covered in school.

Multicultural curriculum transformation does not need to result in an overabundance of new material to teach students. It doesn't mean necessarily dropping required material or the "stuff they need for the test." Teachers can still work from their state's standards by reexamining the way they teach. The transformation does not call for teachers to replace Columbus or the Alamo. It calls for teachers to teach Columbus or the Alamo in a more complete and accurate way and from a broader or non-Eurocentric perspective.

The following are a number of Internet sites (accessed March 15, 2005) that focus on the transformation of curriculum to a more inclusive or multicultural perspective. Most of them contain links to other useful sites.

Multicultural Education and the Internet by Paul Gorski: http://www.mhhe.com/socscience/education/multi_new/

The University of Georgia's Multicultural Perspectives on Mathematical Education: http://jwilson.coe.uga.edu/DEPT/Multicultural/MathEd.html

The Multicultural Pavilion: http://www.edchange.org/multicultural/

Multicultural Review Homepage: http://www.isomedia.com/homes/jmele/homepage.html

Stanford University-SPICE or Stanford Program on International and Cross-Cultural Education: http://spice.stanford.edu/about/index.html

It is true that mandated testing influences curricular development and teaching style—the "testing tail wags the curriculum dog." It is also true that the concepts of multicultural and inclusive educational practices are relatively new. There are many "turf wars" as the variety and range of traditionally marginalized groups struggle for influence, power, and recognition. There are going to be many versions of what multicultural and inclusive education looks like. The key is to always look at it as work in progress because change in the institution of education is slow. Multicultural or inclusive education is a progressive approach for transforming education that holistically critiques and addresses current shortcomings, failings, and discriminatory practices that are historically entrenched in the institution.

Teachers need to present curriculum in the most appropriate way possible and guide students in constructing new, more useful, and fair views of race, ethnicity, culture, society, gender, and sexual orientation.

Precautions and Potential Pitfalls

It would be a mistake to try to standardize what multicultural or inclusive curriculum should look like. Teachers will need to filter all curricular materials and references through their own perspectives to decide what to use and what to modify. It will vary based on the school and the community where it is being taught. The details of the curriculum and practice may change but the main concepts are respect, tolerance, and the elimination of social injustice. These concepts are constant across social strata. It will continue to be up to individual creative teachers to look inside themselves for the strength to develop instructional practices that lead students to find authentic contexts and to examine these topics and the students' role within the concepts.

Sources

Agee, J. (2004). Negotiating a teaching identity: An African American teacher's struggle to teach in a teacher-driven context. *Teachers College Record, 106*(4), 747–763.

Burroughs, R. (1999). From the margins to the center: Integrating multicultural literature into the secondary English curriculum. *Journal of Curriculum and Supervision, 14*(2), 136–155.

Gorski, P. (2004). Multicultural education and the Internet. Retrieved March 3, 2005, from http://www.mhhe.com/socscience/education/multi_new/

STRATEGY 9: Focus on the classroom management factors that best reflect culturally responsive teaching.

What the Research Says

In Brown's 2004 study, 13 urban teachers, ranging from grades 1–12, reflected on their classroom management strategies. These teachers were selected from seven major cities across the United States. The demographics of each teacher's classroom drew from African American, Hispanic, Native American and Asian American students, as well as a wide variety of recent immigrant and refugee students. Among the teachers interviewed there were two Hispanic Americans, one African American, a native Sri Lankan, and nine teachers described as "white."

Their professional experience ranged from 2 to 33 years of teaching. They were selected for the study based on either personal knowledge or information gathered from colleagues regarding their teaching effectiveness. All were recognized as highly effective urban educators. The primary questions used to gather data included

- How do you interact with students?
- How would you describe your management style?
- What works well for you in communicating with students?

Their responses were then compared and contrasted with research on culturally responsive teaching. Participants revealed using a number of techniques supporting the notion that their responses do reflect culturally responsible teaching. The following are the main elements of their management strategies:

- Development of personal relationships with students
- Creation of caring learning communities
- Establishment of business-like, structured learning environments
- Use of culturally and ethnically congruent communicative processes
- Demonstrations of assertiveness
- Use of clearly stated and enforced expectations

Classroom Applications

Culturally responsive teaching means purposely responding to the needs of the culturally and ethnically diverse learners in the classroom. It is a student-centered, student-oriented approach as well as a curricular challenge to go beyond the basics. Culturally responsive teaching uses communicative processes that reflect knowledge of community, family norms, student norms, values, and beliefs. Culturally responsible teaching also uses the knowledge held about teaching and learning to define the responsibility of teachers and the roles of students in the classroom.

Culturally responsible management focuses on the elements and components that involve the ability of the teacher to develop a safe classroom social and academic environment. Students are free to take risks and know that teachers and other students will treat them with respect. This environment features students who agree to cooperate with the teacher and fellow students in the pursuit of academic growth and success. Managing student behavior and maintaining an appropriate learning environment is an art. The teachers in Brown's study offered a number of suggestions reflecting specific areas of management focus.

1. Personalized Relationships, Caring Attitudes, and Mutual Respect Through Individualized Instruction

The most important characteristic described by the teachers was the conscious effort to develop strategies emphasizing personal attention and a relationship with each student. Teachers made it a point to communicate individually with students on academic and nonacademic matters and to genuinely connect to each student's emotional and social persona.

Many urban students lack supervision, attention, understanding, and caring in their homes and communities. Therefore they struggle with inadequate communication processes with adults. This research emphasized that the best urban teachers use warmth and affection to develop relationships with students as pathways to student growth. It was stated that students, "preferred teachers who displayed such attitudes and established community and family-type classroom environments" (Howard, 2001).

Teachers need to take time out of their day to communicate with as many students as they can about nonacademic matters in addition to academic concerns. They need to try to see students in settings outside of the classroom. Mutual respect means taking a personal interest in each student and creating an emotionally safe and secure environment.

2. Building Caring Learning Communities

One of the teachers in the study stated, "It doesn't matter what content you have, or what good curriculum you have, or what exciting lessons you have; if you don't care about students and they know that, you don't have a chance to get to them." Another explained, "You have to get to their heart before you get to their head. The fact that you care makes them see you differently." Another teacher said that, "You have to form a viable social community before they can become a viable learning community." The research emphasized that students and teachers are here to help one another and any behavior that threatens or breaks down this environment and the class values needs to be addressed and discouraged.

Many urban students lead stressful and challenging lives outside the classroom. Often their responsibilities outside of class call on them to make adult decisions about taking care of their brothers and sisters, raising their own families, or working to support their families. Urban students may resent an unequal or unbalanced authoritarian power relationship in the classroom.

A more democratic style of classroom emphasizes cooperation, mutual goal setting, decision making, and shared responsibility. A democratic classroom respects the rights of others and helps students take control over their learning. Spending the time to create this type of environment may be perceived as off-task or noninstructional behavior, yet the establishment of such an environment actually leads to a more productive learning and teaching environment, as well as student engagement and buy-in.

3. Establishing a Businesslike and Highly Structured Learning Environment

The more experienced teachers in this study were forceful in describing their need to establish a business-like learning environment while also managing to maintain mutually respectful relationships with students. Creating clearly stated expectations and enforcing them during the year was described as very important. Expectations for students were highly structured and communicated in detail. No excuses were permitted. Students knew what to expect down to every detail. Students were expected to learn and not to interfere with the rights of others to learn.

4. Establishing Harmonious Communicative Processes

Establishing the rules of discourse or communication requires effort. Differences or misunderstandings in discourse can affect the quality of relationships between teachers and their students. The social interaction styles of some urban ethnic groups or cultures can be misidentified as disrespectful. For example, some Asian cultures use ritualized laughter to maintain harmony and avoid conflicts with authority. Gay (2000) identified certain African American groups who have a social interaction style referred to as "call response." The students may frequently speak while the teacher is speaking as a response to their feelings about a teacher's comments. This is not meant to be rude. In this setting, this can be seen as an entry strategy into conversation through personal assertiveness rather than waiting for an "authority" to give permission (Gay, 2000).

Teachers in this study mentioned that their students needed many opportunities for socialization as a part of instructional interaction. They have a need for verbal interaction during class time. Teachers can create meaningful bonds with students based on genuine social discourse, but teachers need to realize appropriate discourse often needs to be taught.

Good listening skills can also be taught. The power of classroom discourse cannot be overlooked in establishing caring, respectful relationships.

In many situations there may be a mismatch between cultural norms of discourse, and it is up to the classroom teacher to make sense of these mismatches. Culturally diverse classrooms pose unique problems as the student demographics can be different for every class and every school. This issue also can spill into parent-teacher communications. Because every community and school presents a different set of norms and communication styles, teachers must explore the topic within the local setting to help better normalize the elements of discourse in professional interactions.

5. Teaching With Assertiveness and Clear Expectations

One of the greatest weaknesses among new teachers, described in Brown's research, is their lack of confidence regarding assertiveness with students. The least experienced teachers who were interviewed admitted their initial reluctance to establish high expectations for behavior and academic achievement.

A challenging aspect of management plans involves establishing an appropriate balance of power in the classroom. Teachers must maintain authority status and provide students with some decision-making power while avoiding power struggles with students.

Delpit (1995) describes a view held by some ethnic or cultural groups that power and authority are expected to be earned by personal effort and exhibited by personal characteristics. This contrasts with a view held by mainstream middle-class cultures where one achieves authority by acquisition of an authoritative role. A teacher is an authority because he or she is a teacher.

All the beginning teachers in this study described a weak or soft start or a meek and mild approach as the "kiss of death" for classroom management. Students need to know that teachers have standards and expect things of them. Sometimes students don't have anything expected of them anyplace else in their lives. Assertive teachers also need to realize that these types of relationships develop over time.

The researchers also described fear toward students as perhaps the most dangerous reaction by teachers in urban classrooms for failing to establish and maintain an effective management plan. If teachers ignore misconduct, the power balance shifts out of an adult-child relationship into something else that often cannot be recovered once it slips away. Teachers must be assertive in responding to inappropriate behavior expectations to protect the classroom's academic and social environments. Responses must be applied consistently and fairly.

Some may see assertive behavior in conflict with a teacher's efforts to develop democratic opportunities. Democratic decision making should not create a conflict with the standards and rules designed to protect the classroom. However, too much freedom or choice can exceed the students' level of maturity in decision making. All teachers need to develop a level of professional savvy and awareness to strike a balance between control and a cooperative classroom spirit. Experience is the best teacher.

Finally, all the teachers in this study with more than five years of experience established clearly stated expectations and consequences for behavior and used assertive strategies when necessary to reinforce their authority as teachers. They all stressed business-like learning environments with clear expectations for behavior and academic progress. In contrast, the novice teachers reflected on the difficulty they faced because of their failure to establish clearly defined expectations and an assertive stance.

Brown concluded by saying that much of the success by teachers in urban environments depends on their ability to develop positive classroom learning environments through the implementation of culturally responsive classroom management practices. The suggestions presented here offer a good start.

Precautions and Potential Pitfalls

All the strategies here should be seen as guidelines. Human nature demonstrates that every classroom and student mix is going to present different challenges. There are no perfect formulas. Also, urban settings can be very tough on new teachers; teacher retention statistics reflect this. Most teachers need to hit the ground running, with the necessary management survival skills. It is generally better to start firmly and loosen up than to try to get a class back after a weak start.

Sources

Brown, D. F. (2004). Urban teachers' professed classroom management strategies: Reflections of culturally responsive teaching. *Urban Education, 39*(3), 266–289.

Delpit, L. (1995). *Other people's children: Cultural conflict in the classroom.* New York: New Press.

Gay, G. (2000). *Culturally responsive teaching: Theory, research, and practice.* New York: Teacher College Press.

Howard, T. C. (2001). Telling their side of the story: African-American students' perceptions of culturally relevant teaching. *Urban Review, 33*(2), 131–149.

STRATEGY 10: Include multicultural works when developing a quality English curriculum.

What the Research Says

Even with the wide calls for more multicultural texts and literature in secondary English curriculum, teachers have encountered roadblocks to integrating new literature into their courses. Selections do not always hold up well against competition from the great works from more traditional canons. In this context selected multicultural additions often are marginalized. Nontraditional authors do not fit comfortably into the curriculum.

Another concern is that students often distill a curricular march through the more classic selections as a search for "right" answers with little connection to why the works were chosen or how they might connect to a larger purpose. The content finds little or no context or connection to students or other parts of the curriculum. This collected research seeks to discover a more *knowledge-in-action* discourse and current conversation about living traditions. The main concern is that lists of classics, or the selected tradition, predispose curriculum to a more teacher-centered and less student-centered pedagogy. A student-centered approach would strive to include multicultural texts as "curriculum in conversation" and use it as a framework for discussing multicultural literature.

In Burroughs's (1999) research, three teachers' experiences were used as part of a larger study of teacher decision making regarding curriculum involving eight English teachers in 19 classrooms in two high schools. The three teachers featured in the paper came from the same high school, which had a diverse student body with more than 50 percent African American students. Observations were taken over a two-year period as teachers worked, with varying degrees of success and motivation, to integrate multicultural literature into the curriculum.

Of the three experiences, one included very little multicultural curriculum because the structure of her course and her teaching style crowded it out. A second included many multicultural works and changing conversations that put multicultural curriculum as the center of instruction. Another actually created a multicultural curriculum course and changed what were defined as literary works while creating new conversations to analyze them. She expanded what has been traditionally considered literature.

Classroom Applications

The responses of the teachers in the study to the task of creating a more multiculturally inclusive literary curriculum yielded three very different responses. The responses also helped redefine and develop new ways of thinking about what is curriculum and how it should be selected. It showed that changing to a more inclusive curriculum requires more than just selecting multicultural texts and a range of minority authors. While an essential and positive starting point, simply selecting is not enough. For example, teachers in this study expanded the term *literature* to include speeches, myths, plays, and journals, as well as novels and poems.

Beyond making selections, teaching and learning also require thinking about how teachers and students should experience and appreciate the content and its context. Scope and sequence were also seen as important, and the notion of curriculum needed to incorporate some intellectual continuity of discourse as a theme in the construction of curriculum. Teachers in these studies found that the types of student conversations desired began to drive decision making. They found students responded well to some selections and not to others. Adjustments were made.

In the Burroughs study, the least successful teacher only added one multicultural text to her existing curriculum, and students found little evidence of context and relevance to the scope and sequence of the course.

The major problem the teachers in the study encountered was the challenge of providing a scope and sequence without the class time and space to provide it. Teachers found that unlike a college course where literature can be more effectively grouped as a coherent curriculum, high school students lack the background and teachers have a difficult time making connections between time periods and source cultures. The literature range required for high school is too broad, and time is too short.

One of the ways two of these teachers solved the problem was to make textual selection criteria a more explicit part of the classroom conversation. One created a theme called "What is American Literature," which allowed him to move away from a more traditional approach. In the new multicultural literature course, "World Cultures," the teacher created conversations to reflect cultural and individual differences within the classroom as well as within the literature.

As teachers work to broaden the traditional literature canon, it is more realistic and useful to think about restructuring the entire curriculum rather than just adding a new text. Multicultural restructuring requires a look ahead as to how students will experience and use the new information they are given. Context and relevancy need to be considered, and strategies of discourse are very important. Although it was not mentioned in the research, the nature and makeup of each class can interact with curriculum in different ways. Diverse classes mean a variety and range of educational consumers, each with different expectations and mindsets.

Given an opportunity, the three teachers in this study responded to the challenge of inclusion with various degrees of motivation and success. What is clear is that inclusive curricular design is not easy. Giving a voice to traditionally marginalized groups is an art, not a science.

Precautions and Potential Pitfalls

⚠ Restructuring is always a process loaded with workplace politics over funding, department policy, priorities, and so forth. If teachers are not already doing something, somewhere in the future schools and teachers are going to be accountable for their efforts to create an inclusive curricular experience for students. It would be a mistake not to begin to make the effort now. The only question individual teachers have to ask themselves is how are they going to respond to the inquiry about inclusion in their classrooms. They need to begin to develop a multicultural vocabulary when it comes to curricular discussions.

It is always a challenge for a teacher to replace curriculum. There are always worries that the students are going to miss something they need for a standardized test. Keep in mind that politics do play a part, and well-intentioned teachers can encounter resistance from all sides.

Sources

Agee, J. (2004). Negotiating a teaching identity: An African American teacher's struggle to teach in test-driven contexts. *Teachers College Record, 106*(4), 747–763.

Burroughs, R. (1999). From the margins to the center: Integrating multicultural literature into the secondary English curriculum. *Journal of Curriculum and Supervision, 14*(2), 136–155.

Gorski, P. (2004). Multicultural education and the Internet. Retrieved March 3, 2005, from http://www.mhhe.com/socscience/education/multi_new/

2

Including Students With Special Education Needs

You can not put the same shoe on every foot.

Syrus Publilius

STRATEGY 11: *Recognize that different cultures view disabilities differently.*

What the Research Says

 Research on cultural factors and issues affecting families of children with disabilities is relatively new. Parental roles have been conceptualized and changed by professionals over the past three decades. Basically three recent time frames have been defined in this work according to a specific style of approach. Early research emphasized a psychoanalytic approach to parenting (Harry, 2002). This focus indicated that the discovery of a disability was a point of crisis for the family and did not address the impact of culture. During the 1970s, a shift in popular psychology viewed the parents as teachers and sought to educate parents regarding instructional approaches. This approach evolved into the present model, which views the parent as a collaborator with educational professionals. It is in this model that culture plays the biggest role.

Harry's research describes current trends and influences on cross-cultural issues and cross-cultural professional preparation. It identifies a number of culturally important factors for professionals to consider in preparation for meeting the needs of cross-cultural students with disabilities and their families.

Differences in perception can be found in cultural differences in the definitions and the interpretations of disabilities; cultural differences affect family coping styles and responses to disability-related stress. Cultural differences also exist in parental interaction styles, as well as expectations of participation and advocacy. Often different cultural groups have different, and sometimes inequitable, access to information and services; and there can be negative professional attitudes to, and perceptions of, families' roles in the special education process.

Classroom Applications

Teachers need to recognize that a child with disabilities may be viewed differently by a parent from a diverse culture. In certain settings, there can be subtle but powerful ethnocentrism that makes it difficult for mainstream practitioners or researchers to recognize and give credence to non-mainstream family patterns or practices.

The challenge of providing culturally appropriate services can be captured by Atkin (1991), reflecting about black minorities and health and disability services, who said, "Service provision for disabled people usually embodies the views of the provider rather than the user" Atkin calls for research and service provision policies that are informed by, "an account of disability in terms of black people's perceptions without these perceptions being seen as pathological" This principle should be seen as central to the process of decision making about services for minority populations. However, becoming aware and reflecting the "views of the user" is no small task if the service providers essentially do not like, share, or respect those views.

Typically, teachers and other school personnel exhibit mind-set differences based on ethnicity or culture. Also, school personnel's strong identification with the culture of educational professionalism can also present communication barriers, regardless of ethnic identity. Professionals can find it difficult to break the traditional mold of the professional monopoly of information and decision making.

All teachers should develop cultural sensitivity. As more and more students with disabilities are mainstreamed or involved in inclusive programs, instruction should be presented with a strong practical emphasis that requires students to develop and practice an awareness of cultural principles. Often this process begins with personal self-examination, reflection, and awareness of the cross-cultural paradigm. By gaining culture-specific knowledge, which includes effective communication techniques, teachers can enhance their instructional approaches. Teachers should develop a style of nonspecific cultural practice that can lead to a successful professional-parent relationship without being totally familiar with the culture. Teachers should also take advantage of opportunities to learn from parents and other family members and consider using family members in roles that support classroom instruction or school-related activities. Teachers need to develop observation and interviewing skills seen through a culturally sensitive lens.

Precautions and Possible Pitfalls

The limitations of a culture-specific approach, however, include the danger of bias and stereotyping and the inability of the elements presented to define the infinite range of differences among cultural groups. It is important to respect cultural differences but, at the same time, students with disabilities do have specific instructional needs. It is vital that teachers remain sensitive to culture but also balance the educational needs of the student. One aspect of culture should not override the need for an academic modification or accommodation that leads to student learning.

Sources

Atkin, K. (1991). Health, illness, disability and Black minorities: A speculative critique of present day discourse. *Disability, Handicap and Society*, 6(1), 37–47.

Harry, B. (2002). Trends and issues in serving culturally diverse families of children with disabilities. *Journal of Special Education*, 36(3), 131–139.

> ### STRATEGY 12: *Teach all students about disabilities to facilitate the social acceptance of students with special needs.*

What the Research Says

Few can argue that the inclusion of students with moderate and severe disabilities in a general education classroom is a valuable goal that should lead to greater acceptance and understanding of students with special needs in society in general. Also, students with special needs benefit from a wider range of social and academic opportunities. Sadly, in some settings, the idealistic assumption behind inclusion is often undermined. Students with moderate and severe disabilities are often socially excluded from interactions with their peers, particularly during adolescence. Social acceptance is fundamental to the quality of life for all people, including those with disabilities. Sparling's study (2002) sought to determine what barriers exist to inclusion of adolescents with disabilities in their school peer groups.

Sparling conducted a qualitative study surveying 534 high school students (grades 9–12). The goal was to determine factors that affect the social acceptance of students with moderate and severe disabilities at the high school level. The nature of the student's disability, social and cultural influences, and teacher attitude and modeling, as well as adolescent psychology and peer pressure are all cited as issues that affect inclusion. Sparling's survey results found that the social inclusion of students is hampered by several factors, including:

- A lack of knowledge about disabilities, which leads to fear and uncertainty in how to interact with students with disabilities
- Peer pressures, which discourage students without disabilities from interacting with their classmates with disabilities
- School and community culture, which may focus heavily on the values of success and achievement
- The nature of the student's disability, which hampers traditional communication and may also lead to inappropriate social interactions
- Teacher attitude regarding disabilities, which determines the tone of the class and therefore the degree of acceptance of all students

While the survey results revealed that students with special needs are accepted in certain situations at the high school level, there is room for improvement through education and encouragement of nondisabled students and staff at the school.

The survey results indicated that 82 percent of the general education students would help a student with special needs if asked by a teacher or teacher assistant; 10 percent stated they would not; and 60 percent said they would interact more if the teacher or teaching assistant explained how better to relate to students with special needs. Sixty-eight percent of the students in this study responded that students with physical or intellectual disabilities would fit in better socially if students knew more about the disabilities. Again, knowledge appears to be the primary factor affecting social inclusion of students with disabilities (Sparling, 2002).

Classroom Applications

Knowledge is the key to the successful inclusion of students with disabilities. It decreases fear and diminishes the stereotypes associated with people with moderate and severe disabilities and facilitates their social inclusion. Teachers and students can benefit from increased knowledge about the characteristics of specific disabilities, as well as how to best provide instruction for students with those disabilities. In most secondary school settings, students with special needs are assigned to classes by computer, and there may be little support or education provided other than the brief description in the Individualized Education Program (IEP). For the most part, teachers are on their own preparing for the wide range of support students require.

With the wide range of information available on the Internet and the proliferation of books and periodicals dedicated to specific kinds of disabilities, teachers should be able to access concrete information about specific disabilities with relative ease. As always, that information should be considered in light of its source and must be factored against the individual in question. Often teachers will find that armed with a small amount of basic information, they can open a positive dialogue with a student regarding the student's disability. This is particularly effective when determining effective instructional practices and can also serve as a vehicle for helping students develop self-advocacy skills.

Sparling's study indicates that many teachers have a positive attitude toward inclusion, but most expressed concerns regarding the lack of training to effectively teach students with disabilities and classes that included them. The study also identified the greatest concern teachers have regarding students with disabilities—the effect on classroom norms. Most teachers believe they are fair and kind to special education students; however, they need to optimize their knowledge to build better action plans for instruction and to build community in the classroom. They need to anticipate problems and develop potential solutions before issues come up.

Teacher attitude affects and influences how general education students see students with disabilities. A lack of knowledge about how to communicate and the nature of student disabilities lead to fear and decreased acceptance, which affects social inclusion. It's clear that increasing the knowledge of all students can have a positive effect on acceptance.

Educating students about specific disabilities can take many forms. Carefully modeling positive behaviors, informally or formally educating general education students, and inviting individual students to discuss their own specific disabilities can be effective strategies. Engaging in subtle conversations with selected students, peer leaders, and those most receptive, teachers can start to break the ice. Knowledge is the key to inclusion, and teachers are in the best position to use their creativity to develop effective strategies that meet the needs of all of their students.

Precautions and Possible Pitfalls

Teachers need to be cautious that in their efforts to educate students about specific disabilities that they are not embarrassing specific students or making them uncomfortable. Working gradually and focusing on what students do well rather than what they can't do will set a positive tone in the classroom. Research indicates inclusion is a fast-growing educational strategy, and evidence continues to mount in support of the positive effects of inclusive education for all students. Developing sensitivity and implementing strategies that foster successful and effective inclusion are essential. As teachers become better at inclusion they become better overall teachers.

Sources

Glazer, N., & Moynihan, D. P. (1963). *Beyond the melting pot.* Cambridge, MA: MIT Press/Harvard University Press.

Katz, J., & Mirenda, P. (2002). Including students with developmental disabilities in general education classrooms: Social benefits. *International Journal of Special Education, 17*(2), 14–24.

Sparling, E. (2002). Social acceptance at senior high school. *International Journal of Special Education, 17*(1), 91–100.

 STRATEGY 13: Avoid excessive drill and repetition when teaching math.

What the Research Says

 Success in math instruction can depend on a variety of factors. This is particularly true for students with disabilities. In a study of 84 second graders in which 42 were identified as learning disabled, Tournaki (2003) determined that the success of the students with disabilities depended on the type of math instruction they received. The study created three groups of students. The first received pullout instruction in math facts using drill and repetition. The second group received pullout instruction using a strategy approach. The third group acted as a control and received no pullout instruction. Although the nondisabled students improved with both kinds of instructional pullout, the students with disabilities improved their math skills when taught math strategies rather than direct instruction with drill and repetition. When asked to respond to math questions requiring a transfer of math skill, only the students in the strategy group improved their performance (both students with disabilities and those without).

Classroom Applications

 Many teachers believe that the acquisition of math facts is facilitated by time spent on drill and practice. Repetition and speed drills are commonly employed to build mastery. While some students may find these activities helpful, they are often painful and frustrating for students with learning disabilities. Taking the time to teach the strategy behind the math fact may yield a more positive outcome in the long run. Teachers should consider employing a guided instructional delivery where the class moves together through a specific strategy. Students are then given a variety of problems to apply the strategy to. The strategy can be retaught as needed to ensure student success. Often, the same strategy taught from a different perspective or using a different example can enable student understanding.

This approach is supportive of a constructivist view of math that is endorsed by the National Math Standards. These days, students are asked to explain their answers in math assessments as well as provide the correct solution. Beginning that dialogue with a teacher's support, students can explore a strategy as well as how it can be applied in a variety of situations. This will help students develop the logical thinking skills that are essential to higher-level math including algebra and geometry.

Some teachers may choose to take this a step further and invite their students to create their own math questions. Students can then present their questions to each other and explain how to use the strategy to find the correct answer. Student-generated examples don't have the "neat" answers that math textbooks do and may help students become less intimidated about applying math in a variety of settings.

Precautions and Possible Pitfalls

It is important that teachers recognize that some students may never progress to the mastery levels that their nondisabled peers achieve. Regardless of lack of speed, the advantage for the student with a disability is that having learned the strategy, he or she will have the opportunity to approach unfamiliar problems with the strategy in mind.

Source

Tournaki, N. (2003). The differential effects of teaching addition through strategy instruction versus drill and practice to students with and without learning disabilities. *Journal of Learning Disabilities, 36*(5), 449–459.

 STRATEGY 14: Spend more time teaching a few key concepts rather than trying to cover it all.

What the Research Says

 Researchers Eylon and Linn (1988) report that students retain more knowledge cognitively when exposed to a systematic, in-depth treatment of a few topics than they do to conventional narrow treatment of many topics. It is recommended that teachers of all subjects focus on the key concepts presented by their curriculum and spend more time on a limited set of specifically selected knowledge and skills. Students' misconceptions and lack of understanding of basic concepts reflect limitations of mental processing and memory. Ted Sizer, a well-known progressive educator, identifies "less is more" as one of the major principles to guide educational reform (cited in Cushman, 1994).

Classroom Applications

As more and more educators center their curriculum design on state standards and essential elements for instruction, isolating key concepts becomes a natural extension of instructional planning. The first step in that process is articulation with prerequisite and more advanced course instructors to identify the essential concepts presented by a specific course. Teachers can then use this information to identify the key information their courses must cover. When considering students with special needs because of disabilities or language deficits who may not be able to access the entire breadth of the curriculum, it is essential that teachers be mindful of critical concepts when modifying instruction. Once these decisions have been made, teachers can guide students to vital chapters of the textbook to prevent overload and rote learning of non-essential material.

Teachers can encourage students to focus in-depth on specific concepts and their application to a variety of settings by minimizing extraneous detail. For example, students who are able to draw a diagram and label the forces acting upon an object may be more successful than those who memorize a series of position formulas.

Precautions and Possible Pitfalls

 Given the emphasis on standards-based instruction and high-stakes assessment, teachers should be careful to ensure their curriculum meets the requirements outlined by their state and district. Even with standards in mind, teachers shouldn't automatically eliminate potentially interesting learning units or favorite topics. There is a lot to be said for the impact of teacher enthusiasm and passion for specific concepts, topics, and content on student motivation.

Sources

Cushman, K. (1994, November). Less is more: The secret of being essential. *Horace*, *11*(2), 1–4. Available online at www.essentialschools.org

Eylon, B., & Linn, M. (1988). Learning and instruction: An examination of four research perspectives in science education. *Review of Educational Research*, *58*, 251–301.

 STRATEGY 15: Tailor homework to ensure success for students with disabilities.

What the Research Says

Epstein, Munk, Bursuck, Polloway, and Jayanthi (1999) examined homework and the effectiveness of homework communication between parents, students, and teachers. Specific interest in homework came in response to studies that have found that students with disabilities experience more difficulty with homework than do their counterparts without disabilities. Data gathering revolved around a national survey that ultimately included 1,266 general education teachers' responses to relevant questions. The results indicate that several forms of communication, including the use of technology, were found to be highly effective for improving home-school communication.

When students leave class, the teaching and learning environment for doing schoolwork becomes unequal. All students are going home and into their communities to a variety of environments and relationships that are different in many respects. In one home, a student might be supported by college-educated parents, reference resources, the Internet, and a quiet work place. In another home, a parent may work nights at two jobs, and few resources are available. The opportunity to overcome or compensate for a disability in one environment may be optimal and nonexistent in another environment. This means the assigning of homework assignments needs to be well thought out and structured carefully so as not to put any student at a disadvantage. Teachers need to be cognizant of the idea that students with learning disabilities—and sometimes others—may need accommodations in the way homework is organized and structured as a learning device. In addition, parents and the home environment must be active considerations in a successful homework policy.

The results of the Epstein et al. (1999) research indicated that general education teachers perceived several common practices, as well as use of technology, to be highly effective for improving home-school communication about homework for students with disabilities. Among the most highly ranked recommendations were release and mutual planning time, assignment books and logs, parent attendance at meetings and daily monitoring of their child's homework, and use of telephone networks or answering machines to provide remote access to assignments. To this list we can add Web sites and group e-mailing as teachers reach out for greater communication. Each method comes with its own strengths and limitations and needs to be considered on a site-by-site and teacher-by-teacher basis.

Classroom Applications

Teachers use homework to provide additional learning time, to strengthen study and organizational skills, and, in some respects, to keep parents informed of their children's progress. Generally, when students with disabilities participate in the general education curriculum, they are expected to complete homework along with their peers. But, just as students with disabilities may need instructional accommodations in the classroom, they may also need homework adjustments.

It is essential that teachers work as carefully on homework strategies as they do on other parts of the curriculum. Many students with disabilities and their parents find homework challenging, and teachers are frequently called upon to make accommodations for these students. Teachers should ensure students and parents have information regarding policies on missed and late assignments, extra credit, and available adaptations.

Some teachers have found that creating an established homework routine helps students and parents know what to expect. Designing homework that dovetails with material covered in class can help students make positive connections. Ensuring that the homework assignment is achievable is the next key step, as is taking the time to explain the assignment carefully in class. Many teachers find that having students begin homework assignments in class helps clear up any misunderstandings and contributes to student success.

Teachers will find that considering individual homework accommodations and making any necessary modifications to the assignment before sending it home will also help students with special needs be more successful. Depending on the individual needs of the student, teachers may find that providing choice in assignments makes a difference. Adjusting length and time frames can also have positive results, as can adjusting grading criteria as needed.

Teaching homework strategies and skills can help all students and particularly those with learning disabilities who need instruction in study and organizational skills. Teaching students to break down assignments and develop sequential plans for completing multitask assignments can also help. Having a homework rubric that clearly outlines the criteria and grading scale can also communicate homework requirements to both students and their parents. Some teachers offer some credit for work completed on time in addition to the content credit. Others pregrade or check assignments for accuracy and completion and offer revision opportunities before due dates.

Technology can also facilitate homework completion. Although many students keep assignment calendars, teachers who post their assignments on a Web site or telephone homework hotline often find a greater number of students turning in work. Some teachers also use e-mail to contact students and parents about upcoming projects and grades. Teacher Web sites can also be used as a reference source for parents and students on basic study skill techniques as well as links to other useful Web sites.

Precautions and Possible Pitfalls

Even with the most careful planning, organization, and student training, a teacher can only control the homework environment to a point. This means there may be inequities that can't be compensated for, no matter what. There are some schools and individuals who have given up trying to get students to engage in homework. There could be many reasons for this, but inertia continues to exert pressure on students not to do homework. If students don't feel homework is important or meaningful to them, it may take some time, creative effort, and planning to change the climate.

Source

Epstein, M. H., Munk, D. D., Bursuck, W. D., Polloway, E. A., & Jayanthi, M. (1999). Strategies for improving home-school communication about homework for students with disabilities. *Journal of Special Education, 33*(3), 166.

STRATEGY 16: *Spend the time to develop and use a variety of assessment strategies.*

What the Research Says

Researchers Campbell and Evans (2000) examined 309 lessons designed by 65 preservice teachers and discovered that few teachers implemented the concepts they had studied in their educational measurement coursework. This lack of conceptual implementation made it difficult to link the curricular goals to the instruction and ultimately to student mastery. The researchers also noted that more than 23 percent of the lesson plans had either omitted or contained nonobservable instructional objectives. Although 113 plans included rubrics for assessments, only 8 were completely developed. Consistent scoring methods were also a deficit area.

Although these teachers agreed that assessment was an important aspect of instruction (81 percent), they seemed to view instruction and assessment as separate facets of a lesson rather than parts of the same process to inform future instruction. The researchers noted that the technical aspects of test construction were demonstrated but remarked that the inferences made about student progress were weak.

Classroom Applications

Assessment should be the specific research that drives future instruction, not simply a summary of student mastery. There has never been a better time to find information on assessment and instructional practices. State framework writers, educational agencies, special interest groups, and parent organizations heavily analyze course content. Many of these analyses produce not only content outlines but pedagogical and assessment suggestions and guidelines. In addition, most textbook publishers (who design their books based on the same documents) provide instruction and assessment strategies connected to their books' content. Many also provide alternative assessment suggestions for teachers working with students who require modifications, accommodations, or enrichment.

Most subject content frameworks are now accessible via the Internet, and most textbooks come with ample support material. In addition, many teachers use assessment strategies that connect to skills required on those standardized tests students are taking. Teachers should analyze and use them all within their personal instructional context.

The resources are available, yet the dilemma for most teachers is deciding which to use. Some of these resources offer more valid and reliable information. The key is finding a secure bridge between instructional goals, classroom instruction, and assessment. Teachers should survey as much information as they can access before synthesizing their own strategies.

The strategy for most teachers is to construct the unit or lesson in a complete package with equal attention to goals and objectives; instructional delivery systems; and fair, reliable, and valid assessment strategies. If assessment is considered and addressed before beginning instruction, teachers will find peace of mind and security as they move the students toward final assessment. They'll know what skills their students will need to be successful, and they always have that in mind. In this way, they can always make adjustments to instruction, quicken or slow the pace, simplify or rework instructional trouble spots, or tweak the assessment if necessary, particularly for those students who require additional supports.

Precautions and Possible Pitfalls

For many teachers, politics plays a heavy role in assessment. Teachers often find themselves split between using assessment instruments and strategies that prepare students for standardized testing formats and using more authentic assessments. A solution to this dilemma is to develop a variety of assessment options for students. Many teachers find that providing choice for their students contributes to student buy-in as well as making for more stimulating and less repetitive grading for the teacher.

Source

Campbell, C., & Evans, J. A. (2000). Investigation of preservice teachers' classroom assessment practices during student teaching. *Journal of Educational Research*, *93*(6), 350–356.

 STRATEGY 17: Offer positive and constructive feedback rather than criticism.

What the Research Says

At least three studies (Daiker, 1983; Dragga, 1986; Harris, 1977) have shown that often teachers do not praise students' writing enough. Daiker, Kerek, and Morenberg (1986), "found that the vast majority of comments (89.4%) cited error or found fault; . . .

10.6% of them were comments of praise" (p. 104). In a separate study focusing on a sophomore honors English class at a public high school in the Midwest, students were polled as to what types of teacher comments on their writing provided the most help while encouraging them to improve as writers. The students responded that they prefer to see comments worded in a positive manner on their papers. Although there is value in knowing where errors were made, they wanted advice on how to correct their mistakes (Atwell, 1987). This positive and constructive feedback can translate to improvement in student writing.

Classroom Applications

Most teachers believe that writing is a process and that the focus with student writing is improvement and development over time. The more specific a teacher can be with comments on students' work, the more students will be able to accurately identify the next step and area for growth. Teachers who provide thorough explanations of and deserved praise for what students have done well, as opposed to marking only what is wrong, inspire their students to continue to work on their writing.

Teachers must also look at their own commenting style. They need to notice if they tend to comment only on form or content. Are the ideas the student is proposing considered? If the objective is to improve over several drafts, then certainly grammatical errors such as spelling and punctuation should not comprise the majority of a teacher's comments. These parts of writing are important, but can be revised in a later draft, after the student has the content problems ironed out. Do students know what is right with their work as well as what needs to be done to correct mistakes? Telling students to be more specific has little or no meaning for them if they do not know which part of their text needs to be more specific.

Teachers can model effective correction techniques by using a generic or teacher-created writing sample that the class corrects as a group. By combining this approach with a rubric, students can make the connection between what is required and what a specific writing sample demonstrates. Some teachers also find that having a series of drafts on different topics collected and then inviting students to choose their best one to revise helps to prevent boredom and burnout in student writing.

Precautions and Possible Pitfalls

Teachers need to be careful not to use praise that is too general or of a patronizing nature. At the beginning of a course, teachers should go over their specific commenting style with students and whether they will use symbols as well as written comments. Teachers should make sure students understand what these symbols mean. In addition to written comments, teachers should talk to students on a regular basis about their papers and encourage students to ask questions if the comments they are given aren't clear.

Sources

Atwell, N. (1987). *"In the middle": Writing, reading, and learning with adolescents.* Portsmouth, NH: Boynton/Cook.

Bardine, B. A. (1999). Students' perceptions of written teacher comments: What do they say about how we respond to them? *High School Journal, 82*(4), 248–249.

Daiker, D. (1983, March). *The teacher's options in responding to student writing.* Paper presented at the annual Conference on College Composition and Communication, Washington, DC.

Daiker, D. A., Kerek, A., & Morenberg, M. (1986). *The writer's options: Combining composing* (3rd ed.). New York: Harper.

Dragga, S. (1986, March). *Praiseworthy grading: The researcher's perspective.* Paper presented at the annual Conference on College Composition and Communication, New Orleans, LA.

Harris, W. H. (1977). Teacher response to student writing: A study of the response pattern of high school teachers to determine the basis for teacher judgment of student writing. *Research in the Teaching of English, 11,* 175–185.

STRATEGY 18: Communicate student progress early in a course, but avoid using formal grades to do so.

What the Research Says

Researchers Lechner, Brehm, and Zbigniew (1996) investigated four ninth-grade classes concerning the effects of giving grades at an early stage of knowledge acquisition. To show the effects of early marking, the four classes were separated into two groups. Both groups received computer-aided instruction and were graded after every step. The first group did not get to know about their grades, while the second group was informed of their grades. The achievements of the groups were compared on the basis of the grade after every step and on a final test. Students who knew their marks did slightly better on the interim tests. In contrast, on the final test, students who did not know their interim grades did noticeably better. They were not pushed by the pressure of marks. They used additional work to develop self-control. In this way, they dealt with the issue of their learning needs, they understood it profoundly, and they achieved at higher levels.

Giving grades early in the learning process may stimulate students to participate actively in their lessons, but it may undermine achievement in the long run. Previous research provided evidence that some students learn because of anxiety over grades or because they get good grades with a minimum of effort. Giving grades early is not beneficial for students who require more time to understand things. They tend to be afraid of saying something wrong and of getting bad grades. Early grading should not be viewed as a judgment of a student's knowledge. It should be viewed more as informative rather than as judgmental.

Classroom Applications

There is no question that constructive feedback helps students assess their own learning and academic performance. Yet the impact of grade-specific feedback can lead to difficulties in some students. Because early grades can easily frustrate students who are not interested in a particular topic or even the course content, teachers should avoid giving grades at an early stage of learning. Although for some students early grades can promote rapid success, in other cases this leads to students resting on their laurels. During the period students are acquiring new knowledge, teachers should use grades sparingly and use other forms of feedback to communicate student performance.

Teachers need to remember that not all feedback needs to be evaluated with a specific grade. The process of learning and putting together a product is increasingly seen as more important than the finished product itself. Simply checking off a step or stamping work as completed before moving on to the next can be enough incentive to keep instruction and learning moving, particularly if it is accompanied by constructive feedback.

Alternative forms of feedback could include written teacher comments, rubrics, oral commentary, and peer evaluation. The more specific and constructive feedback a student receives, the more he or she will understand what step to take next.

Precautions and Possible Pitfalls

Although the emphasis is on feedback rather than grades, teachers should not stop all assessment during the early stage of learning. First, students need assessment to evaluate or at least estimate their own achievement. Several smaller quizzes can also reduce the anxiety that can accompany one larger exam. In addition, teachers will always find some students who are entirely motivated by grades. Providing these students with some sort of measure may help them gauge their progress while keeping them motivated.

Source

Lechner, H. J., Brehm, R. I., & Zbigniew, M. (1996). Zensierung und ihr einfluß auf die leistung der schüler [Influence of marks on student achievement]. *Pädagogik und Schulalltag, 51*(3), 371–379.

STRATEGY 19: Ensure students receive appropriate instructional or assessment accommodations.

What the Research Says

Ysseldyke et al. (2001) studied four local education agencies (LEAs) in Maryland and Kentucky and reviewed the IEPs of 280 students to determine how the recommended accommodations were being used on statewide tests. The researchers concluded that 84 percent of the students were using accommodations on assessments that were also used during instruction and were appropriate for the individual students based on the disability and its severity.

Ysseldyke et al. (2001) advised that IEP teams should carefully consider the individual student's needs prior to recommending accommodation for instruction and assessment. The most common accommodations were reading aloud to students with reading difficulties, taking dictation for students with writing difficulties, calculators for students with math difficulties, and extra time or breaks. The researchers found that a minimum of one month of using the specific accommodations was advisable before having a student use that accommodation during the assessment.

Classroom Applications

Sometimes, in an effort to help students who have disabilities, IEP teams will recommend every accommodation that comes to mind. Kindly, they reason, "Wouldn't every student benefit from extra time so he or she doesn't feel pressured? Preferential seating because it's near the teacher? Material read aloud because he or she will receive extra attention?" and so on. Although these things look good on paper, receiving an accommodation can be embarrassing for a student, particularly if it is one that the student doesn't really need or benefit from.

Based on the collected data, the IEP team suggests appropriate accommodations, but it is up to the student and the teacher, working together and keeping the lines of communication open, to ensure that the accommodation is really serving the needs of the student. Teachers need to offer the specific accommodation to the student as the IEP requires, but they need to take it one step further by noting if the student benefited. An easy way to do this is simply to note on the top of any given assignment or assessment what accommodations were offered, what ones were used, and the outcome. For example, if the student needed a calculator to complete the class work, the teacher can note "Calculator used" along with the score. These data will help the student and the IEP team to determine which accommodations actually benefit the student.

Precautions and Possible Pitfalls

 Teachers need to take care not to make the mistake of not offering a student an accommodation that is specified in the IEP even if they feel the student doesn't need it. Failure to comply with the IEP, a legal document, may result in a lawsuit. The student may choose not to use the accommodation, and that is up to him or her. Teachers should make a note of what was offered and if the student refused. The only way to change the accommodations noted in an IEP is to request a meeting to amend the IEP.

Source

Ysseldyke, J., Thurlow, M., Bielinski, J., House, A., Moody, M., & Haigh, J. (2001). The relationship between instructional and assessment accommodations in an inclusive state accountability system. *Journal of Learning Disabilities, 34*(3), 212–221.

 STRATEGY 20: Be aware of potential bias when considering the recommendations of the Student Study Team.

What the Research Says

In two southern elementary schools, multidisciplinary teams were evaluated to identify specific issues that could explain the disproportionate number of African American students who were placed in special education (Knotek, 2003). This study documented that, although teams of professionals rather than single evaluators are required by law in an effort to avoid the bias in the referral process, unfair trends can still develop. The study found that bias was more prevalent when students from lower-socioeconomic families or students with behavior problems were discussed. If the students discussed had either of these issues, the discussion became very subjective and the team recommendations became, "more reflexive and less reflective" (Knotek, 2003, p. 13). It is important for teams to track their recommendations and look for emerging patterns of referral. Although some students may require similar services, it is vital that each student be considered individually.

Classroom Applications

Most schools use a Student Study Team (or Child Study Team or Multi-Disciplinary Team, etc.) to identify students in crisis or in need and brainstorm services and potential solutions. Often the team consists of a special education teacher, a counselor, a psychologist, an administrator, and a general education teacher. Each of these professionals brings a different perspective to the table as individual student needs are discussed. Participants need to pay close attention to the process and monitor the referrals that comprise the team's history. Trends should be noted—is every student of color being referred to the same program, or is every Latino student being referred for language assessment? Notes should also be taken as the team makes suggestions for accommodations for the student in the current placement. Are the same recommendations made routinely (change in seat, an after-school tutoring program, peer helper, etc.), or are they creative and flexible in their suggestions?

It is also important that the team keep records of the students discussed and the suggested follow-up. Whatever actions the team recommends should be assigned to a specific person to implement, and a date should be set for review.

If a trend is noticed, the team should meet outside of its scheduled Student Study Team (SST) meeting to discuss the trend and evaluate whether the issue requires further exploration. It is vital that a trained facilitator who is not part of the team help with this discussion to guard against it becoming a personality attack. Teams gain personalities of their own and can effect change as a group if all members are committed to the process.

Precautions and Possible Pitfalls

 Each professional comes to the table with his or her own set of experiences and perspectives as a result of those experiences. It is not uncommon for a new program or a new teacher who is trying a different approach to suddenly become the panacea for all students who are having problems at a school. Although this should be rare, be careful to note if the team is filling a new class or program blindly rather than considering each case individually.

Source

Knotek, S. (2003). Bias in problem solving and the social process of student study teams. *Journal of Special Education*, 37(1), 2–15.

 STRATEGY 21: Focus on classroom process before course content to increase time on task.

What the Research Says

 Sardo-Brown (1996) reviewed the current literature to examine new teacher planning. The study examined how two first-year teachers planned their first and second years of teaching. She also asked the teachers to compare and contrast the differences between the years. The two teachers in the study were selected based on their competency within their graduate education classes and because both had obtained employment in secondary schools right out of teacher education.

The most noticeable difference in first- versus second-year planning was giving management issues a higher priority than content during the early weeks of school. In their second years, both teachers dedicated much more time to process by setting up and teaching rules, procedures, and class structure along with developing early rapport with their students. Both teachers planned major adjustments to their methods of assessment, and both sought out more time-efficient strategies and planned to use more high-level assessment methods as learning strategies.

Classroom Applications

Although the primary task of any teacher is to impart knowledge of specific content to students, experienced teachers know that creating a positive learning environment is a crucial first step in the teaching process. Spending the time to clearly teach classroom procedures and learning process is time well spent. This is particularly important when working with students with disabilities or limited English skills. Creating a safe and predictable classroom environment helps all students feel comfortable and contributes to a more positive teacher-student interaction. Knowing what to expect and what is expected of them helps students function more effectively in class. Misbehavior becomes a choice rather than an incidental product of confusing instructions or inconsistent procedures.

Teachers need to do the "science" it takes to determine what happens when real students meet a teacher's management and instructional strategy. The classroom experience is ongoing research. Each data collection through assessment or observation tells the teacher what he or she needs to work on the following week. Just as assessment informs instruction, teacher reflection on process contributes to effective change and ultimately more time spent on instruction and learning.

Many teachers find that covering basic procedures clearly and in detail helps reduce time spent off task and in transitions. Developing clear guidelines for turning in homework, restroom visits, pencil sharpening, asking questions, working in groups, cleaning up, and so forth can make all the difference in time spent on instructional content. Some teachers find it helpful to use similar procedures to other teachers on site so that students have a measure of consistency.

Precautions and Possible Pitfalls

 It's clear from the research that time on task is a large factor in teacher development. As teachers become more experienced, their classroom procedures and processes become more streamlined and students spend less time in transitions and more time learning. For most teachers, there are few shortcuts from the first days in class to the end of the year.

Focusing on how students can be helped should be the priority. Teachers should avoid making too many changes at one time if previously established procedures must be adapted. In addition, teachers should consider inviting students into the dialogue in determining how things should be done in their classroom.

Source

Sardo-Brown, D. (1996). A longitudinal study of novice secondary teachers' planning: Year two. *Teaching & Teacher Education, 12*(5), 519–530.

STRATEGY 22: Consider using
Universal Design for Learning
principles when designing lessons.

What the Research Says

Just as Universal Design in architecture allows the builder to incorporate design principles that benefit a wide range of people while saving the expense of retrofitting an older building, Universal Design for Learning (UDL) allows an instructor to create a lesson that meets the broad range of student needs. Researchers Scott, McGuire, and Shaw (2003) noted that college instruction differs from K–12 instruction in three main areas: legal mandates regarding access, specification of curriculum, and preparation of instructors. Their research reviewed the changes in postsecondary education over the past decades and traced the origin and development of UDL. Changing demographics require changes in postsecondary instructional practices. The July 2000 American Council on Education reported that two thirds of at-risk students go on to college, and many of these students qualify for special education services through Section 504 of the Rehabilitation Act and the Americans with Disabilities Act. Most typically, these students are given accommodations based on their disabilities (extended time, note taker, etc.). Changes in the student population have occurred simultaneously with changes in technology, professorships, and the idea that the student is a consumer.

From this starting point, Scott et al. (2003) extensively reviewed the literature on UDL and identified nine basic principles that can be implemented at any level:

1. Equitable Use: Instruction is designed to be accessible to students with diverse abilities.

2. Flexibility in Use: Multimodal instruction provides for student choice.

3. Simple and Intuitive: Instruction is designed in a predictable manner with unnecessary complexity eliminated.

4. Perceptible Information: Instruction is communicated effectively to each student regardless of student's sensory abilities.

5. Tolerance for Error: Teacher anticipates variations in student pace and skills.

6. Low Physical Effort: Instruction minimizes nonessential physical effort.

7. Size and Space Appropriate for Use: Instruction considers student's body size, posture, mobility and communication needs.

8. A Community of Learners: Instruction promotes interaction and communication between students.

9. Instructional Climate: Teacher is welcoming and inclusive, and has high expectations for all students.

Classroom Applications

Although this body of research focused on postsecondary instructional practice, the nine principles identified are essential elements of quality instruction at any level. In K–12 teaching, it can be easy to rely on what teachers are told to do: "Teach the adopted text, give extended time because the IEP says to, etc." Yet, the difference between an adequate teacher and an excellent teacher has always been and will always be the ability to inspire significant learning in his or her students. By considering the nine elements of UDL, teachers can endemically create a classroom environment that supports all students.

Consider the idea of equitable use. With the availability of technology increasing, teachers can provide copies of lecture notes and homework assignments online for ease of student access where assistive technology can be used by students with diverse needs. This ties in to the second element of flexibility in use. Most teachers know that variety in instruction (group work, labs, lecture, video, skits, etc.) enhances student interest; however, adding student choice into assignments encourages students to learn the way they learn best.

Keeping material simple and intuitive seems obvious, yet many students can't make the connections that their classmates do. By providing clear and written explanations, rubrics, and expectations for assignments, teachers can eliminate many points of confusion for their students. In keeping with this is the idea that the information should be perceptible to the students. Teachers need to consider how students are able to communicate (e.g., in another language, with a hearing aid, with Braille) and design instruction that is accessible for all students.

Tolerance for error implies that teachers recognize and accept the fact that their students have different skill levels. Teachers can support students by building in opportunities for skill development (practice) and feedback on a regular basis. By allowing students to turn in parts of larger projects as they go along, teachers can ensure that students are progressing appropriately.

The idea of low physical effort invites teachers to understand that some students have physical limitations that may impede their progress. For example, some students are unable to handwrite at length and may be more successful with a word processor. This concept dovetails with the idea of size and space. Students come in all shapes and sizes, and teachers need to be cognizant of the needs that accompany their students. Many desks are too small for the suddenly tall adolescent and completely inaccessible for a student in a wheelchair. Even classroom design can influence student success. Some students thrive in small groups; others benefit from linear rows to help focus their attention. Teachers need to keep these needs in mind as they design their instruction to facilitate the growth of a community of learners. By encouraging students to work together and by maintaining ongoing dialogue about the content, teachers can facilitate student communication and learning. Many teachers encourage students to use chat rooms or instant messenger to set up study sessions to keep the communication going.

All of these concepts come together to create an effective instructional climate that emphasizes respect and diversity. Teachers can reiterate the importance of attitude through activities, modeling, and discussion.

Precautions and Pitfalls

At first, implementing all nine elements in instructional design to create a universally accessible curriculum may seem daunting. Yet the secret to effective implementation lies in awareness and adaptability over time. Teachers need to realize that small steps add up, and creating a universal design is an ongoing process based on reflection, student achievement, and feedback.

Source

Scott, S. S., McGuire, J. M., & Shaw, S. F. (2003). Universal design for instruction. *Remedial & Special Education*, 24(6), 369–380.

STRATEGY 23: *Encourage students to set process goals when learning new technology.*

What the Research Says

Schunk and Ertmer (1999) studied goal setting when teaching students to use computers. The study found that students who set process goals felt they learned more effectively than those who set product goals. Students in the process condition (i.e., learning state) believed that they were more competent in performing specific tasks than the students in the product condition. Achievement results showed that process condition students indeed were more successful than the students in the product condition in performing HyperCard tasks.

It's beneficial to teach students to set learning goals for different reasons, and different kinds of goals have different effects. Goal setting can affect students' achievement and motivation, and it can affect how students regulate the use of their thoughts, actions, and feelings. Students can use the goals they set as standards for assessing their own progress. Goals focusing on the learning process emphasize the strategies that students use in acquiring skills or information. In contrast, goals focusing on the product of learning emphasize outcomes or results, such as how much was accomplished and how long it took.

Classroom Applications

One of the steps in learning new technology is identifying current skills and developing goals for areas of deficit. Part of teaching self-advocacy skills and helping students to internalize learning is to have students regularly set process goals when acquiring new knowledge or skills. Some teachers use a think-aloud procedure and write on the board to model for students how they should design process goals. Students might begin by brainstorming possible goals individually or in groups. Then they can write their goals in clear and simple terms. Students benefit from periodic reflection and updating their goals to meet their current skills. Teachers should not underestimate the rigorous and challenging learning that technology requires when making progress toward a more primary goal or product.

Some situations require as much or more time to learn how to perform a task than does actually performing the primary task. Teachers should help students make realistic time estimates and include the technology learning curve. Some examples of process goals that may need to be mastered before finishing a project or activity are

- Student groups need to learn a spreadsheet and graphing program to be able to manage and summarize the data from a statistics experiment. They may need to complete a tutorial and manipulate a few small data sets before looking at their own data.
- Students using a laptop computer with a physiology-sensing capacity need to learn the accompanying software to make their experiment and data collection fully functional.
- An earth science group accessing a weather and climate Web page is required to learn the Web page's specific programs to manipulate its temperature and rainfall data.
- Students from a high school located near a university need to master the university library's digital library and e-journal access online catalog to acquire the background information for their research papers.
- Students need to evaluate many curriculum-related Internet sites to assess which sites are the most accurate and useful. A graphics program needs to be learned to develop overheads and slides to be used in an English presentation.

Precautions and Possible Pitfalls

 Teachers should not just let students copy general process goals for learning to use computers or other technology. Self-generated specific goals are more personally meaningful to students than teacher-imposed goals.

Source

Schunk, D., & Ertmer, P. (1999). Self-regulatory processes during computer skill acquisition: Goal and self-evaluative influences. *Journal of Educational Psychology, 91*(2), 251–260.

STRATEGY 24: *Create scaffolds to help students learn complex skills and procedures.*

What the Research Says

Walberg (1991) suggests that in science it is especially useful for students to struggle with interesting, meaningful problems that can stimulate discussion about competing approaches. This idea can be stretched to include all disciplines. He recommends using what he calls comprehension teaching, more commonly called scaffolding, which involves providing students with temporary support until they can perform tasks on their own. Based on Vygotsky's (1978) concept of the "zone of proximal development," scaffolding is recommended for teachers to build from what students can do only with temporary guidance from a more competent person, gradually reducing and eventually removing this support as students become independent thinkers and learners who can perform the task or use the skill on their own. The zone of proximal development refers to the area within which the student can receive support from another to successfully perform a task that he or she cannot perform independently. Scaffolding is an excellent method for developing students' higher-level thinking skills (Rosenshine & Meister, 1992). Scaffolding is a strategy for gradually and systematically shifting responsibility and control over learning and performance from the teacher to the student.

Classroom Applications

 Through a variety of methods (e.g., observation, listening, tests), a teacher can assess students' abilities to perform and not perform important skills or tasks independently. Testing a student's ability to perform or not perform these skills or tasks with assistance from another enables one to conceptualize the student's zone of proximal development. Teachers can use a scaffolding approach for skills and tasks that are within the student's zone. Scaffolds can range from a simple hint, clue, example, or question to a complex sequence of activities that begin with teacher-centered approaches (e.g., explaining, demonstrating) but end as student-centered (e.g., self-questioning, self-monitoring).

The example that follows is a scaffolding approach for teaching students to construct graphic organizers of text they have read. It is a complex sequence of steps that uses scaffolding to shift from teacher direction and control of creating graphic organizers to student self-direction and self-control over making them.

1. Show and explain a variety of traditional examples of graphic organizers, such as flow charts, concept maps, and matrices, made by both professionals and students.

2. Tell students what graphic organizers are and when, why, and how to use various types of them. One source (Jones, Pierce, & Hunter, 1988/1989) provides information on why and how to create graphic organizers to comprehend text, and it provides illustrations of a spider map, a continuum or scale, a series-of-events chain, a compare-contrast matrix, a problem-solution outline, a network tree, a fishbone map, a human interaction outline, and a cycle. Another source focuses on concept maps and Vee diagrams (Novak, 1998).

3. As class work or a homework assignment, give students a partially completed graphic organizer to finish on their own. Give students feedback on their completions. For students of different abilities, a variety of graphic organizers can be used. For the more capable student a larger number of spaces are required; for the less capable student, fewer blanks or less complex responses may be acceptable.

4. Assign class work or homework that requires students to complete an empty graphic organizer structure entirely on their own. Give students feedback. For students with disabilities, consider allowing them to work with a partner prior to completing the assignment on their own.

5. Assign class work or homework requiring groups of students to create their own graphic organizers. Teachers should assign the groups heterogeneously, paying close attention to personalities as well as abilities. Give students specific criteria or rubrics for constructing and evaluating graphic organizers. Sample criteria include (a) it is neat and easy to read, (b) ideas are expressed clearly, (c) ideas are expressed completely but succinctly, (d) content is organized clearly and logically, (e) labels or other strategies (colors, lines) are used to guide the reader's comprehension, (f) main ideas—not minor details—are emphasized, (g) it is visually appealing, and (h) the reader doesn't have to turn the page to read the words.

6. Once their graphic organizers are completed, the individual groups show their graphic organizers to the other groups, which critique the

graphic organizers and give them feedback based on the criteria identified above. Teachers should supplement the feedback as needed.

7. For homework, students develop graphic organizers completely on their own, using the identified criteria. Group members give each other homework feedback on the extent to which they met the established criteria.

8. Finally, students are expected to be able to create and critique their own graphic organizers, and support from others (students and teacher) isn't needed.

Precautions and Possible Pitfalls

To use scaffolding effectively, it is vital for teachers to consider issues such as what types of support to provide and when and what order to sequence them in, and to figure out the criteria for deciding when it is time to reduce or withdraw support from students. It is also very important to make sure scaffolding attempts are truly within the students' zone of proximal development. If they are below this area, activities will be too easy because the students can really do them independently. If they are above this area, no amount of scaffolding will enable students to perform independently because the skill or task is too difficult given the students' prior knowledge or skills.

Sources

Jones, B. F., Pierce, J., & Hunter, B. (1988/1989). Teaching students to construct graphic representations. *Educational Leadership, 17*(2), 20–25.

Novak, J. (1998). *Learning, creating, and using knowledge: Concept maps as facilitative tolls in schools and corporations*. Mahwah, NJ: Erlbaum.

Rosenshine, B., & Meister, C. (1992). The use of scaffolds for teaching higher-level cognitive strategies. *Educational Leadership, 49*(7), 26–34.

Vygotsky, L. S. (1978). *Mind in society: The development of higher psychological processes*. Cambridge, MA: Harvard University Press.

Walberg, H. (1991). Improving school science in advanced and developing countries. *Review of Educational Research, 61*(1), 25–69.

 STRATEGY 25: Focus on instructionally centered communication when working with students with learning disabilities.

What the Research Says

Researcher Cook (2001) examined the effects of teachers' attitudes toward their included students with disabilities based on and in relation to the severity of the disability. Using prompts denoting the attitudes of attachment, concern, indifference, and rejection, 70 inclusive classroom teachers responded by nominating three students who represented each of the attitudes. Further analyses produced predictors, based on a theory of instructional tolerance and a model of differential expectations, that students with severe or visible disabilities were significantly over-represented among teachers' nominations in the indifference category. Also, students with mild or hidden disabilities were significantly over-represented among teachers' nominations in the rejection category. Results were interpreted to mean that teachers tend to form different attitudes and expectations for their included students with disabilities depending on the severity or visibility of students' disabilities. Included students are at risk for receiving inappropriate educational interactions.

Classroom Applications

Communication between teachers and students should be primarily focused on instructional interaction. Unfortunately, with some groups and individuals, teacher communication shifts from an instructional interaction focus to a behavioral or disciplinary interaction. This moves the communication away from the more appropriate and purposeful types of educational interactions that further student learning. Although it is normal for teachers to become attached to some students and place others in categories of concern, indifference, or total rejection (as described in the research), all teachers must make an effort to consider carefully before making judgments, interpreting situations, and forming attitudes regarding individuals.

Inappropriate perceptions of disabilities can negatively influence the attitudes teachers hold toward their included students with learning disabilities. This results in changes in the frequency, duration, expectation, and quality of teacher-student interactions. More time may be spent on redirecting behavior and correcting students than is spent on teaching them.

Bias and stereotyping can be very subtle and come from a place very deep in the subconscious. Once teachers think about it or are made aware of it, they can develop personal action plans to change these patterns of behavior and implement more objective ways of creating meaningful and effective educational interactions. This is particularly important for a student who may have the same disability as another student but whose behavior (or needs) is completely different.

Self-education is the key. Sharing ideas with trusted colleagues or talking it over with a favorite special education teacher allows teachers to see themselves and their included students in a more objective light. Once they are made aware of their possible bias or stereotyping, they are glad to replace those ideas with more useful and accurate lenses with which to view students. This new outlook can lead to a more positive focus on instruction and student learning.

Precautions and Possible Pitfalls

There is no question that students with disabilities often have behavioral issues that complicate the instructional process. The important point is to keep the communication between the teacher and the student focused positively on learning as much as possible. Bias and stereotyping are very personal, and only new knowledge frees teachers from these notions. Developing more accurate and useful ways of seeing students is a powerful strategy for increasing teachers' abilities to meet the needs of all students, but this process takes time. Just as teachers are aware that small gains in their students can lead to significant growth over time, they need to extend a similar perspective to their own personal growth as educators.

Source

Cook, B. G. (2001). A comparison of teachers' attitudes toward their included students with mild and severe disabilities. *Journal of Special Education*, 34(4), 203–213.

STRATEGY 26: Encourage students with disabilities to develop positive interpretations of their academic performance.

What the Research Says

Some students fall into patterns of negative thinking when it comes to academic performance, falsely thinking that because they didn't do well in a class in the past, they can't be successful in that subject area. However, extensive research shows that students can learn to control their own academic destinies. When focusing on students' attributions for success and failure, there are four common reasons people give for their successes and failures: ability, effort, task difficulty, and luck (Alderman, 1990).

Attributions can be divided into two dimensions: stable-unstable and internal-external. Stable-unstable refers to how consistent the attributions are over time—that is, the extent to which a person uses the same types of reasons to explain his or her success or failure over and over again (stable), or whether the person gives one kind of reason on one occasion and another type of reason another time (unstable). For example, a student says solving acceleration problems in calculus is always too difficult for him (stable), but in physics some velocity equations are easy for him and some are too difficult (unstable). Stable arguments are often harder to influence. They are often avoidance arguments and are used to avoid work the student feels threatened by. Older students tend to form defensive *stable* arguments to avoid potential failure situations.

Internal-external refers to how a person assigns responsibility for his or her successes and failures—inside or outside the self. For example, a student says she didn't do well on her exam on the Spanish-American War because she didn't study enough (internal). She says she didn't do well on her English essay because her family interfered with her study time (external). She says she received a high grade on her second English essay because she was lucky (external).

Students' explanations of their successes and failures have important consequences for future performance on academic tasks. Research shows there are four common ways students explain their successes and failures (Alderman, 1990):

1. Effort ("I could do it if I really tried.")

2. Ability ("I'm just not a good writer.")

3. Luck ("I guessed right.")

4. Task difficulty ("The test was too hard.")

Attributions are related to the expectations about one's likelihood of success; the judgments about one's ability; the emotional reactions of pride, hopelessness, and helplessness; and the willingness to work hard and self-regulate one's efforts.

Classroom Applications

Teachers need to help all students develop positive associations and beliefs about learning. By actively addressing a student's self-talk when it comes to academic performance, teachers can help students create a more productive outlook. Students who see a relationship between their effort and their success are more likely to use learning strategies such as organizing, planning, goal setting, self-checking, and self-instruction. Alderman's (1990) "links to success" model, which follows, is designed to help at-risk students develop attributions that will motivate them to succeed.

1. Help students develop proximal goals, which are short term rather than long term, specific rather than general, and hard (but reachable) rather than easy. For example, the goal, "This week I'll manage my time so that I have three extra hours to study," meets the basic criteria, but for the student with disabilities, the time frame for proximal goals may need to be shortened. Depending on the student's individual needs, consider goals measured in 15-minute, half hour, class period, or daily increments. Teach students to anticipate and overcome obstacles, monitor progress while goals are being pursued, and evaluate whether they achieved their goals at the end of the specified time. Adding a statement like, "I'll know whether I accomplished this goal by writing down how much time I study and comparing that to how much time I studied last week," can make a difference in how a student progresses. Teach students to anticipate possible obstacles to achieving their goals by identifying circumstances that might get in their way and decide ahead of time how they will deal with them. For example, "If I get invited to a party Friday night, then I will move my study time to Saturday afternoon and skip going shopping." As part of their reflective model, if students don't achieve their goals, teach them to determine why and evaluate what they could do differently next time.

2. Embed learning strategies in subject-specific instruction. Effective strategies, like summarizing and clarifying, emphasize meaningful learning and can be used across subjects and situations. Ineffective approaches, such as repetition, which tends to emphasize rote memorization, can be difficult for students with learning disabilities—particularly those with short-term memory issues.

3. Provide students with successful academic experiences. Have students evaluate their success in achieving their proximal goals and focus on their individual growth and learning ("How much progress did I make?") rather than performance ("What grade did I get?") as the goal.

4. Give students feedback on why they succeeded or failed and help them arrive at the appropriate explanation. Was an answer incorrect, incomplete, or was there a careless mistake? Make sure students understand why an answer is incorrect. Ask questions such as, "What did you do when you tried to answer that question or solve that problem?"

Precautions and Possible Pitfalls

Feelings of helplessness can be created over a period of time through the belief that failure is related to lack of ability, so it is important for students to internalize that their ability can improve if they use effective strategies and make appropriate efforts. This is particularly important when dealing with students who have a heightened sensitivity to their own learning issues. Students want to resist being put in positions of failure and are often more motivated by fear of failure than by the "new" strategies for success. Occasionally, and usually with older students, some efforts simply won't work. Don't give up on all students because a few have given up on themselves.

Source

Alderman, M. K. (1990, September). Motivation for at-risk students. *Educational Leadership*, 48(1), 27–30.

 STRATEGY 27: Use instructional strategies that support the specific needs of students with attention deficit hyperactivity disorder.

What the Research Says

 Researchers Zentall, Moon, Hall, and Grskovic (2001) determined that the most effective instructional strategies for students with attention deficit hyperactivity disorder (ADHD) include personal attention, opportunities to be in leadership or helper roles, and the use of preferred activities as incentives. Teachers who employed these strategies reported fewer issues with behavior. The least effective instructional strategies were those that took away or withheld activity.

Classroom Applications

Effective instructional approaches for students with ADHD begin with a thorough understanding of the disorder. Stimulation through social interactions and activity-based lessons are effective with students with attentional deficits. Teachers should avoid lengthy spans of seat time and sedentary work. The use of hands-on and manipulative activities is also more effective with many students with disabilities and may enable them to be successful. Providing students with opportunities to move around the classroom can also be helpful. Allowing individual students to run errands, hand out papers, clean the board, or help out in the classroom can help reinforce appropriate behavior.

Students with ADHD may experience greater difficulty in starting and organizing tasks. So teachers should consider breaking assignments down into smaller pieces and checking for understanding at regular intervals. This strategy of *chunking* curriculum benefits all students, not just those with disabilities.

Students with ADHD can be a real pleasure to have in class. These students have an energy and enthusiasm that, when harnessed, can create the most dynamic of lessons. These are the students who will volunteer for kinesthetic activities like role-playing, skits, mock trials, and so on. They will ask questions that stimulate class discussion and often enjoy debate.

Teachers should consider the classroom environment and how it supports or interferes with the needs of a student with ADHD. For example, a classroom near a heavy student traffic area (drinking fountain, restroom, etc.) may prove to be very distracting for the student; he or she may require preferential seating to help minimize the distraction. Conversely, a classroom that is designed for student movement and group activities is an ideal setting for a student with ADHD.

For a teacher working with students with ADHD, the first person to seek out for support may be a veteran special education teacher who has a thorough understanding of the students' IEPs. Consulting a special education teacher to help plan activities and lessons can be a tremendous resource. He or she can also provide helpful hints in dealing with discipline issues, preferential seating, and the importance of presenting clear, specific, and simple directions.

Precautions and Possible Pitfalls

Be careful to avoid traditional behavior modification techniques like restricting participation and withholding privileges when working with a student with ADHD. These approaches may seem reasonable and in keeping with classroom rules and consequences but ironically contribute to an increase in negative behavior rather than a decrease.

Teachers need to be wary of the punitive aspects of their management systems and try to frame consequences in a positive light. For example, rather than keeping a student with ADHD in at recess, a teacher may choose to reward positive behavior with a first-in-line pass. The more the teacher is organized and uses straightforward and concise classroom rules and procedures with consequences clearly stated, the more likely the students will succeed.

Source

Zentall, S. S., Moon, S., Hall, A. M., & Grskovic, J. A. (2001). Learning and motivational characteristics of boys with AD/HD and/or giftedness. *Exceptional Children, 67*(4), 499–519.

3

Cultivating Gender Sensitivity

As long as the differences and diversities of mankind exist, democracy must allow for compromise, for accommodation, and for the recognition of differences.

Eugene McCarthy

 STRATEGY 28: *Open the dialogue with students regarding gender equity issues.*

What the Research Says

 Weiner's (2002) research suggests that men and women's equality issues have dropped off the radar of educational policy, especially in urban schools. Weiner feels gender has been marginalized to a point where those concerned are seen as "missing the bigger picture" within the needs of urban school reform. In her research Weiner explored gender equity, reform, and urban school research from a number of perspectives. First, she looked at the academic literature and quickly moved toward her personal experience dealing with P.S. 3, her daughter's school in Greenwich Village, New York City. She looked at gender bias through the eyes of a parent, teacher, and researcher.

Wiener found gender issues in curriculum and instruction, parent representation, classroom management and discipline, classroom discourse, faculty, and leadership. She found parents and teachers agreed that schools should take a hard look at how they lived up to their charge of opposing sexism. However, she felt that P.S. 3 and other urban schools lacked the institutional ability to carry out improvements. She felt that time was the limiting factor and schools do not have the time to deconstruct gender issues. She writes, "It literally takes time to conceptualize an inquiry, to think about what you take for granted, to look closely at what you assume or hypothesize about a situation or a group of students. . . . The irony is that even planning how to do things takes time, which many teachers do not have" (Weiner, 2002).

In conclusion, she worries that multicultural education is seen as a genderless concern and that race and class are adequate issues in and of themselves. She sees the urban school's bureaucratic structures as institutionalized barriers to achieving gender equity.

Classroom Applications

Gender is a complex issue in education. As a topic for reform, it has ranged from a focal point to a marginalized, peripheral matter depending on its current context and political climate.

Mothers are still the parent of choice for the practical maintenance of the educational setting for their children. According to Weiner's (2002) research, what information exists supports the idea that fathers are very distant from day-to-day maintenance of home-school relationships. Working or career-oriented mothers often work two jobs, one recognized as "work," and the job as a parent, not recognized as work. Chances are home-school contacts are going to be female.

Classroom discourse, management, and discipline are often dominated by the socialization and behavior of boys. Girls are often short-changed in these settings. Because of this they are often robbed of the teacher's time and effort. Gender inequalities take time to be uncovered. It is difficult to analyze school life and professional interactions. Because of cultural conditioning the obvious can be overlooked. It also takes time to reflect on the individual subliminal personal bias a teacher might bring to the classroom. Deconstructing gender regimes requires insight and effort. It competes with other dominant topics of educational reform. Often a teacher's time is dominated by operational concerns, not curricular or instructional concerns during noninstructional time. Gender equity is often overlooked.

Curriculum, if not carefully screened, can reinforce gender stereotypes or perpetuate stereotypical roles. In the described research, the author proposed a highly regarded staff development program to help teachers incorporate nonracist and nonsexist literature into their classrooms. Although the principal responded by starting a reading program and personally selected the books, the program was dropped when she left the school. The researcher felt some faculty saw this program as an intrusion into instructional decision making. This is a symptom of deeper management and teacher problems, but the situation illustrates how institutional bureaucracy can sabotage efforts. Unless a teacher "buys in," the program does not exist.

Caring teachers can't wait for top-down programs to challenge the difficult tasks surrounding gender-sensitive instruction. If it is not part of the mainstream reform efforts such as multiculturalism or class, it needs to be become a personal effort on a teacher's part to modify his or her own classroom practices so as not to reproduce gender inequities.

The first step in this process is to identify the present condition. Teachers can address the issue of gender equity in the context of their content area. For example, history teachers can invite students to explore the historical role of women. Math teachers may want to discuss the numbers of males to females enrolled in classes. Home Economics teachers may bring up issues of gender specific roles in society. This discussion can lead to student recognition of gender issues and pave the way for further dialogue.

Precautions and Possible Pitfalls

 Gender roles are not defined by academics. They are a product of various cultures and societies. Teachers have to be able to avoid direct power struggles over gender ideology or philosophy with students. A teachers' job is to get students thinking, not necessarily to tell them what to think.

Sources

Weiner, L. (2002). Nitpicking: An exploration of the marginalization of gender equity in urban school research and reform. *The Urban Review*, 34(4), 363–380.

Freeman, D. (1998). *Doing teacher-research: From inquiry to understanding.* New York: Heinle & Heinle.

STRATEGY 29: Support male and female students differently during school-to-school transitions, as gender can influence their needs.

What the Research Says

Generally, school transition research supports the notion that negative outcomes, such as decreases in self-esteem and academic motivation, occur for a number of students during school-to-school transitions (elementary school to middle school and middle school to high school). Akos and Galassi (2004) investigated gender and race as variables in sixth and ninth grade students' psychological adjustment, including student perceptions of transition difficulties and connectedness to school following a recent change in schools.

The students in this study came from one middle school and one high school. The results of Akos and Galassi's research suggest differences by gender for feelings of connectedness to middle and high school following the transition. Eccles et al. (1993) suggested that girls suffer greater losses in self-esteem compared to boys during the transition to middle school. Suggested reasons for this center on a difference in peer bonding between boys and girls and girls' early maturation. The combination of physical and social transitions may heighten the negative outcomes of school transition.

Hirsch and Rapkin (1987) report that girls experience greater depression than boys over the transition period from elementary to middle school. Girls frequently reported a lack of assistance with social needs, whereas boys reported feeling a lack of academic support.

During high school transitions, it was noted that boys exhibited more concern with the increased length of classes, participating in sports, and violence from gangs. Girls, on the other hand, expressed more general concerns and greater social and academic concerns.

Hispanic American students perceived the transition to middle school as significantly more difficult than did white and African American students. Akos and Galassi (2004) also found that minority status also might intensify negative transition outcomes. They found that urban settings of high poverty and crowded classrooms can also intensify the negative transition outcomes.

Gutman and Midgley (2000) investigated the transitional effects on African American students and found significant academic decline from elementary to middle school. It was suggested that African American students showed greater decreases in grade point average (GPA) and increased dislike of school after the elementary to middle school change. African American students remained steady over junior high to high school transitions, while whites showed a slight decline and Hispanic students faced steep declines with some rebound toward the end of the year.

Classroom Applications

School transitions play an important role in the developmental trajectory of students. The very individual and personal transformation periods students undergo during puberty and school changes are extensive and can be educationally disruptive and upsetting to the student. Transition periods are frequently associated with declines in academic performance, academic motivation, extracurricular participation, and perceived support from school personnel.

Encouraging extracurricular activities can help. Classes like band and yearbook foster a sense of identity and belonging. Schools might also look into programs such as link crew (teaming veteran students up with students new to the middle or high school setting), field trips, home rooms, and reverse- or cross-age tutoring to help ease the transition period. Teachers who open their classrooms early and keep them open at lunch and after school may provide a safe harbor for students who would welcome a familiar space.

Precautions and Potential Pitfalls

Typically, students move from smaller schools to larger schools. They also move from situations where they are usually known by many students and staff to situations where they are known by only a small group of teachers and students. They often feel isolated in the larger pool of individuals. This can also make it difficult for teachers to get to know their students well. In the rush to deliver instruction, teachers should not lose touch with their students as individuals. Teachers should take more time with transitioning students to personally connect to them. The faster they connect the sooner they can relax and focus on learning.

Sources

Akos, P., & Galassi, J. (2004). Gender and race as variables in psychosocial adjustment to middle and high school. *The Journal of Educational Research, 98*(2), 102–108.

Eccles, J., Ubriaco, M., Reese, A., Gara, M., Rothaum, P., & Haviland, M. (1993). Negative effects of transitional middle schools on students' motivation. *Journal of School Psychology, 30,* 41–57.

Gutman, L. M., & Midgley, C. (2000). The role of protective factors in supporting the academic achievement of poor African American students during the middle school transition. *Journal of Youth and Adolescence, 29,* 223–248.

Hirsh, B., & Rapkin, B. (1987). The transition to junior high school: A longitudinal study of self-esteem, psychological symptomology, school life, and social support. *Child Development, 58,* 1235–1243.

STRATEGY 30: *Become aware of the traits of gifted females.*

What the Research Says

In "Behind the Mask: Exploring the Need for Specialized Counseling for Gifted Females," Ryan (1999) relies on a literature review for support and proceeds on a single premise. The main argument revolves around the idea that gifted children, particularly females, create a mask of conformity to hide their giftedness, individuality, and uniqueness. Gilligan, in 1982, hypothesized that girls at the ages of 11 or 12 are pressured by society to lose their innate personalities and take up traditional female roles. Clark (1983) further adds to the discussion by studying the transitions gifted females experience throughout their maturation. Clark suggests, "The gifted adolescent girl has the combined burden of dealing with the expectations of traditional role models and suppressing her considerable intellectual abilities to avoid success." Indirectly girls also fear being seen as different or exhibiting unfeminine traits within peer groups and school culture. Societal norms often value sexual attractiveness and beauty over academic achievement.

These external pressures produce internal conflicts in gifted females, and girls are at particular risk for emotional instability because of the mixed messages they receive from family, peers, and school staff. For girls who accept mainstream society's expectations and hide their intelligence, a loss of self-esteem and a lower self-image often follow. As a result, "By adulthood, it is likely that the majority of gifted women will settle for far less than their potential" (Noble, 1987).

The research finds that mental health professionals and schools generally ignore the needs of gifted females, so gifted young females form a subculture of silence. The research identifies a common misconception that the gifted require no special services or consideration. Being gifted comes with unique emotional challenges, and gifted girls need assistance in illuminating the somewhat predictable negative consequences of their giftedness.

Kerr (1985), Clark (1983), and Dabrowski and Piechowski (1977) invite teachers to consider girls who demonstrate the following traits as gifted:

- A sharp wit that is often used as a coping and defense mechanism
- An unusual degree of sensitivity to the feelings and expectations of others
- Heightened feelings of self, even at a very young age, often accompanied by a strong sense of being different from the rest of the world
- High idealism and a passionate sense of justice; higher morality than others her age, often higher than society in general

- Emotional supersensitivity along with great emotional depth; high expectations of self and others, often leading to perfectionism
- The need for abstract values and actions to complement each other

The research calls for enlightened and specialized counselors who are aware of the special needs and the strengths of this population. The needs of gifted females and their parents are unique, and they need help in learning more about themselves and their conflicts with the world. Without adequate understanding, counselors cannot help gifted females understand the "gifted female experience."

Classroom Applications

One of the problems with giftedness is measuring or assessing the characteristics of being gifted and talented. Most of the characteristics are much easier to observe than measure, and the criteria are almost always controversial and subject to various forms of political biases. Every school and district has a system for the inclusion of the gifted and talented into a local program or category of student.

To identify gifted girls in the classroom, teachers really must draw from multiple criteria. Rather than rely on test scores alone, teachers should be alert for behaviors that indicate giftedness. Some general guidelines for detecting talent in gifted girls (Smutny, 1999) include

- *Academic behaviors*—Student reads voraciously and retains what she reads, communicates ideas well both verbally and in writing, possesses superior abilities.
- *Conceptual abilities*—Student explores issues from multiple points of view.
- *Creative behaviors*—Student expresses unusual, out-of-the-ordinary points of view; demonstrates special ability in the visual arts; shows promise in performing arts (music, drama, dance); and manifests improvisational ability in a variety of contexts.

Teachers should also be aware of the special challenges that gifted girls face: low self-esteem; apathy, based on resignation or feelings of inferiority; fear of taking risks; exaggerated concern about being accepted among peers; ambivalent feelings about talent; and conflict between cultural identity and school achievement. Often, collecting information from a range of sources is even more important for gifted girls from diverse student populations and from lower socioeconomic backgrounds because these factors add unique stresses to their school achievement.

It is not surprising that peer pressure to underachieve is strong in many culturally diverse settings. In addition, many girls do not respond well to the competitive nature or structure of some instructional settings. Gilligan's research on the moral psychology of women demonstrates how girls adopt an ethic of caring and how it conflicts with the competitive structures of the classroom. Many culturally different and low-income students experience the act of academic achievement as a betrayal to their social group.

Once identified and internalized, teachers can adjust their instructional strategies and personal and classroom discourse to help meet the needs of the gifted female. Teachers can help them learn more about themselves, help them recognize their true nature, and help them identify their conflicts within the world they live.

Precautions and Potential Pitfalls

Teachers need to be careful not to overplay their role in changing the lives of gifted females. The task is to create inclusive learning and teaching environments for gifted females and a range of other traditionally marginalized groups. Teachers need to adjust their teaching styles so they do not perpetuate teaching behaviors that lead gifted females to the problems identified in the research. In addition, teachers need to be aware of the negative issues that can result and be ready to seek additional assistance from school support personnel as student needs dictate.

Teachers of older students, high school and above, need to realize that personalities and behaviors can be very entrenched. Teachers must consider their time with students as *works in progress*. Teachers need to keep their goals and expectations reasonable and avoid adding to the damage with unreasonable strategies and expectations.

Sources

Clark, B. (1983). *Growing up gifted* (3rd ed.). Toronto: Merrill.

Dabrowski, K., & Piechowski, M. M. (1977). *Theory levels of emotional development* (Vol. 1). Oceanside, NY: Dabor Science.

Gilligan, C. (1982). *In a different voice: Psychological development* (Vol. 1). Cambridge, MA: Harvard University Press.

Kerr, B. (1985). *Smart girls, gifted women*. Columbus, OH: Ohio Psychology Publishing.

Kline, B., & Short, E. (1991). Changes in emotional resilience: Gifted adolescent females. *Roeper Review, 13,* 118–120.

Noble, K. (1987). The dilemma for gifted women. *Psychology of Women Quarterly, 11,* 367–378.

Ryan, J. R. (1999). Behind the mask: Exploring the need for specialized counseling for gifted females. *Gifted Child Today, 22*(5), 14–17.

Smutny, J. F. (1999). Understanding our gifted. *Roeper Review, 11*(2), 9–13.

STRATEGY 31: Work to prevent inequities between male and female students' class participation.

What the Research Says

Many studies report that male students participate more in class than their female counterparts, and that teacher behaviors contribute to this pattern (Bailey, 1988; Biklen & Pollard, 1993; Sadker & Sadker, 1994; Sadker, Sadker, & Steindam, 1989). Male students also receive more attention and more specific feedback from teachers and are more likely to receive praise for the intellectual content of their answers. When teachers do not wait for more than five seconds for student responses, they inadvertently favor aggressive male students. Often teachers are unaware of their own discriminatory behaviors until someone calls it to their attention. Teachers may not believe they are responsible for bias in the classroom and may blame society or the students themselves for inequity.

In Lundeberg's (1997) study, 48 preservice teachers (21 men and 27 women) were involved in trying to answer the questions: How do preservice teachers' perceptions of gender interactions compare with actual gender interaction data; do prospective teachers become aware of the limits of their own perceptions in detecting inequities in classroom interaction; and what strategies do preservice teachers propose to ensure equity?

These preservice teachers were all enrolled in sections of an Educational Psychology class. Gender interaction patterns were recorded and researched using a variety of techniques, both in their classes and during outside field experiences. Seventy-three percent said they would promote equity and make a conscious effort to ensure equity in seating, lab work, cooperative groups, and athletic activities, as well as ensure equity in curriculum content and language use. One quarter of the teachers said they would collect data to monitor gender bias (videotape, outside observers). One fifth said they would become more aware of seating arrangements, pairing of males and females. Several planned to use inclusive language to switch gender roles for demonstrations, cleanup, and so forth. The majority of these teachers discussed the need to collect data and monitor classroom interaction to ensure equity in their future classrooms.

Classroom Applications

Teachers need to believe that gender bias exists and address it as part of their instructional design process. Teachers may find that informal action research can alert them to subtle biases they may not be aware occur in their classrooms. Videotaping a teacher's interactions or having someone observing a teacher's teaching can help address subtle gender biases. Teachers can use this information to make appropriate changes to instructional strategies and classroom discourse. For some student populations, teachers may want to address the issue of gender equity as a part of a class discussion.

Precautions and Possible Pitfalls

 Males and females have acquired their behaviors and roles over time. They need to be taught how to recognize gender bias in their own lives. There are many students who are so comfortable in their roles that they resist changing. In these cases, teachers may consider keeping their equity goals as part of a hidden curriculum.

Sources

Bailey, G. D. (1988). Identifying sex equitable interaction patterns in classroom supervision. *NASSP Bulletin*, 72, 95–98.

Biklen, S. K., & Pollard, D. (1993). *Gender and education. Ninety-second yearbook of the national society for the study of education* (part 1). Chicago: University of Chicago Press.

Lundeberg, M. A. (1997). You guys are overreacting: Teaching prospective teachers about subtle gender bias. *Journal of Teacher Education*, 48(1), 55.

Sadker, M., & Sadker, D. (1994). *Failing at fairness: How America's schools cheat girls*. New York: Scribner.

Sadker, M., Sadker, D., & Steindam, S. (1989). Gender equity and educational reform. *Educational Leadership*, 46(6), 44–47.

STRATEGY 32: *Consider how students sometimes treat female teachers differently than male teachers.*

What the Research Says

Miller (1997) interviewed 16 women from three teacher education programs in New England to learn about their experiences as female student teachers and to acquire insight into the gender issues in female student teachers' lives. More than half the women interviewed spoke of being demeaned and objectified. One of the most evident gender issues coming from the study was male high school students' harassment of female student teachers. They told stories of how the cultural habit of viewing women as sex objects affected the environment in which they began teaching.

An in-depth interviewing technique was used to gather information related to specific incidents and how these related to their lives and what it was like as a female to student teach. The predominant complaint centered on how male students felt entitled to exert power in a school context and demean and dehumanize female student teachers through objectification. Other male students were often mute or provided open support to these behaviors.

Their behaviors were described as a power struggle between genders. Male students, who, especially in secondary schools, were relegated to lower power relationships, grabbed control by transforming the recognized authority in the room to a powerless object of their discourse. Language became their weapon.

Classroom Applications

Teachers must develop ways to first become aware of gender issues embedded in management, curricular, and discipline issues and then become more cognizant of the gender factors within their specific context. Many factors can arise from deeply rooted sexist attitudes, both within the teachers themselves and within their students.

There are culture-driven gender issues that female teachers must confront in their own thinking. Miller (1997) pointed to a critical juncture during the middle school years in which girls either learn to be honest about what they see and know around them or deny what they see and know. The researcher found when girls confront individuals or institutions in their lives, they risk losing relationships with parents, teachers, and friends. If they remain silent, girls are more likely to maintain peaceful relationships with the same people. Most girls choose silence. When these women make the transition from student to teacher, from dependence to independence, from passive to active initiator, they need a reservoir of support to draw from. There is a residue from growing up female in this culture, and this residue can show up again at this vulnerable time of learning to teach.

Another problem lies within potential supporting collaborators. Not everyone in the support context may possess enough insight, experience, or empathy to help. Not everyone has the insight to recognize potential gender issues.

Precautions and Possible Pitfalls

Teachers should not overreact and make every sexist remark, look, or comment their own problem. Teachers should pick their battles carefully and tread lightly as some of these entrenched attitudes are invisible to the students themselves. In all likelihood each incident will need to be treated differently, and a different strategy will be needed.

Source

Miller, J. H. (1997). Gender issues embedded in the experience of student teaching: Being treated like a sex object. *Journal of Teacher Education*, *48*(1), 19–28.

STRATEGY 33: *Address gender issues in the classroom to increase student success and confidence.*

What the Research Says

Research from a study by Good and Brophy (1987) found that teachers give male students greater opportunities to expand ideas and be animated than they do females. In addition, teachers tend to reinforce males for general responses more often than they do females. Further, beginning teachers need to be cognizant of the tendency to give more and better feedback to males than to females (Sadker & Sadker, 1994). Previous studies by Fennema and Peterson (1987) indicate that, although female students learn best cooperatively and males learn more easily through competition, it is noteworthy for teachers to give all students opportunities to participate in both learning modes.

Classroom Applications

Before looking further into gender issues, all teachers need to be familiar with Title IX of the Education Amendments of 1972. Title IX forbids discrimination or segregation of students by gender in school programs, courses, and activities. Most people familiar with Title IX think of its legislative implications as specifically to support equal opportunities for girls in sports. The reality is that the law provides equal opportunities for girls and boys at school.

Teachers need to examine their own biases with regard to gender differences and the ways this attitude might impact their teaching. Having a colleague observe class while keeping track of the number of times female students versus male students are called on, whether the interaction is different with boys than girls, and what types of questions and instructional strategies are used with girls compared to boys are all helpful questions to address in bringing biases to the forefront and discussing ways to improve.

One way to provide opportunities for success is to provide learning strategies for all students. For example, to make sure every student has equal opportunities to answer questions in class the teacher could have 3x5 cards with each student's name printed on it. During a question and answer session, the teacher can shuffle the cards and draw out a card. The teacher then calls the name of the student on that card to answer the question. Once the student answers the question or verbally participates in a discussion, the teacher can make a mark on the card to record that student's participation. This same system can be used to assign students to cooperative learning groups as well as to assign specific roles within that group (investigator, recorder, etc.)

Teachers should find guest speakers from both genders and diverse populations. Females and males in nontraditional roles can become role models for students as well as help them visualize those careers in the future.

Teachers need to experiment with and implement strategies that are sensitive to the caliber and equality of interaction of each student. They need to provide occasions for every student to participate actively in his or her own learning and build opportunities for all students to take leadership roles.

Sources

Fennema, E., & Peterson, P. (1987). Effective teaching for girls and boys: The same or different. In D. C. Berliner & B. V. Rosenshine (Eds.), *Talks to teachers* (pp. 11–125). New York: Random House.

Good, T. L., & Brophy, J. E. (1987). *Looking in classrooms*. New York: Harper & Row.

Sadker, M., & Sadker, D. (1994). *Failing at fairness: How America's schools cheat girls*. New York: Scribner.

STRATEGY 34: Be prepared for subtle gender bias in academic situations.

What the Research Says

Career Strategies for Women in Academe considers the current status of women in higher education. It examines women's roles in academe and provides insights and advice on avoiding the subtle gender bias found in academic situations. In addition to citing the most current research, Collins, Chrisler, and Quina (1998) include women's personal accounts with inserts of "success stories and cautionary tales." While focused on women in higher education, the message can be applied to women teaching in K–12 situations as well. Student gender differences bring a range of perceptions toward female teachers.

Classroom Applications

Many of the factors that contribute to negative ratings of women faculty appear to be beyond their control. Certainly students come to college and secondary classrooms with gender-role expectations that are difficult to modify. These expectations permeate society. Often they are so commonplace they are invisible unless someone calls them to attention.

Society as a whole is evolving slowly, but women faculty members can do several things to arm themselves against unfairly negative student evaluations, perceptions, and assessments. Some of these suggestions may not fit an individual woman's personality or ideology. Indeed, it's not fair that women professors/teachers have to be concerned about gender-stereotyped expectations. However, because those expectations do exist, it may be helpful for those who want to build an academic career to know how to try to work around them:

- Discuss gender roles with students. Many students are able to change their perceptions once they recognize what those perceptions are.
- Sharing educational expertise is often a positive way to communicate that competence to students early in the semester.
- Consider the effects of wardrobe on the first impression students receive. More professional attire may help communicate competence. This is particularly true for teachers who appear younger.
- Some teachers may find using a professional title (Dr. or Professor) helps communicate professional expertise and may facilitate students' early impressions.
- While female teachers are often nurturing, they should be wary of communicating too much flexibility as their first task is to educate their students. Support, both emotional and academic, may be offered to facilitate a student's learning but should not be the primary communication or interaction.
- Setting appropriate boundaries for assisting students helps maintain a professional profile. Office hours help communicate accessibility yet ensure that students do not take advantage of a willingness to offer extra assistance.
- Solicit student feedback as part of the ongoing reflection process. Structure the evaluation process for the most usable results. Review course or unit objectives and invite students to reflect on their own learning. Then encourage students to offer constructive criticism for expanded learning opportunities or greater coverage of problem areas.

Precautions and Possible Pitfalls

Every setting presents a different context for gender sensitivity. Taking time to better define how the gender roles are played out in that context is essential before choosing an avenue of response. Consider each class as its own community and choose the approach that best meets those individual needs.

Source

Collins, L., Chrisler, J. C., & Quina, K. (Eds.). (1998). *Career strategies for women in academe: Arming Athena* (pp. 151–152). Thousand Oaks, CA: Sage.

4

Including
Students Who
Are Sexual
Minorities

*The price of the democratic way of life is a growing appreciation of
people's differences, not merely as tolerable, but as the essence of a rich
and rewarding human experience.*

Jerome Nathanson

**STRATEGY 35: *Create a classroom
environment of safety and respect.***

What the Research Says

Approximately 1 in 10 of the students served by public schools
will develop gay and lesbian identities before graduation
(Cook, 1991; Gonsiorek, 1988). Sexual orientation, however,

appears to be established prior to adolescence, perhaps from conception, and is not subject to change (Gonsiorek, 1988; Savin-Williams, 1990). The social stigma surrounding homosexuality discourages many gay and lesbian teens from discussing the confusion and turmoil they may feel about their emerging identities (Friend, 1993). Adding to this sense of confusion and the isolation they may feel, it should not come as a surprise that gay and lesbian youth are "two to six times more likely" than heterosexual teens to attempt suicide. While gay and lesbian teens account for 30 percent of all completed suicides among adolescents, they comprise only 10 percent of the teen population (Cook, 1991).

Classroom Applications

Adolescence is a difficult time for most students. Academic challenges often are overshadowed by personal issues—particularly those surrounding sexual identity. While gay and lesbian youth face many of the same changes with regard to social, biological, and cognitive development as their heterosexual peers, misconceptions and stigmas often add to the stress and turmoil that many gay and lesbian youth struggle with daily.

The physical and emotional safety of every student in class is the cornerstone of instruction. When students feel safe, they are able to take risks in class by asking questions to enhance their learning. Teachers of middle and high school students need to provide a safe and harassment-free environment. Students can be very cruel to each other, and this seems to be heightened more so during adolescence. Not allowing derogatory words (dyke, homo, fag, etc.) or comments in class is a start. If a teacher does not address these negative comments, the gay or lesbian student can feel further alienated and alone. Silence from the teacher is often interpreted as tacit agreement with what is being said. Because homosexuality appears to be one of the last bastions of "acceptable" discrimination, gay and lesbian youth may feel more isolated and withdrawn than heterosexual students. These perceptions of inferiority can lead to poor self-esteem, substance abuse, sexual promiscuity with the opposite sex (to "conceal" their true feelings), and possibly suicide. Teachers should not tolerate students calling each other by racial, ethnic, or religious slurs; they must not tolerate comments of a negative nature to gay and lesbian students either.

Precautions and Possible Pitfalls

Just because a teacher doesn't have a student (or students) declaring that he or she is homosexual doesn't mean there are no gay or lesbian students in the classroom. Research studies estimate 1 in 10 people are homosexual, so it stands to reason that in a class of 30 students, a teacher might have three who are struggling with sexual orientation issues. Don't assume if no one is coming forward to complain about harassment or name calling that the problem doesn't exist.

Students may pose questions to the teacher about homosexuality (Is it okay? Why are some people heterosexual and some people homosexual? etc.). It is not advisable to get into a discussion of right and wrong, okay or not okay. However, telling students that *every* person is entitled to respect, acknowledgement, and acceptance is not only okay, it sets the stage for an optimal learning environment.

Sources

Cook, A. T. (1991). *Who is killing whom?* (Issue Paper No. 1). Washington, DC: Respect All Youth Project, Federation of Parents and Friends of Lesbians and Gays, P.O. Box 27605, Washington, DC 20038.

Friend, R. A. (1993). Choices, not closets: Heterosexism and homophobia in schools. In L. Weis & M. Fine (Eds.), *Beyond silenced voices: Class, race, and gender in United States schools* (pp. 209–235). Albany, NY: State University of New York Press.

Gonsiorek, J. C. (1988). Mental health issues of gay and lesbian adolescents. *Journal of Adolescent Health Care*, 114–122.

Savin-Williams, R. C. (1990). Gay and lesbian adolescents. *Marriage and Family Review, 14*, 197–216.

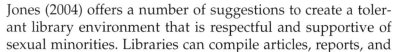

 STRATEGY 36: Access libraries to provide a more inclusive collection for sexual minorities.

What the Research Says

Jones (2004) offers a number of suggestions to create a tolerant library environment that is respectful and supportive of sexual minorities. Libraries can compile articles, reports, and Web sites as well as fiction and nonfiction books to help adults and teens understand sexual minority issues and their effect on teen development. These teens have social, emotional, and health concerns that heterosexual teens don't. Libraries should be safe, respectful, and tolerant environments that are supportive of diverse sexual identities. Libraries can provide resources that help teens understand diverse sexual orientations. They can help them conduct their own searches and find reviews of relevant literature.

Classroom Applications

Just as teachers strive to provide a variety of resources that address different cultures, religions, political beliefs, and so forth, they should make the effort to include sexual orientation as an aspect of diversity. Local and school libraries are often a valuable source of these materials. The following are some online resources on the subject:

- The Gay, Lesbian, and Straight Education Network (GLSEN) at http://glsen.org is an organization focused on safe and effective schools for diverse students.
- Gay Straight Alliance Network at http://www.gsanetwork.org is an organization facilitating Gay Straight Alliance Clubs in schools.
- Human Rights Campaign at http://www.hrc.org is the largest gay and lesbian organization.
- Parents, Families and Friends of Lesbians and Gays at http://www.pflag.org is a site that promotes the well-being of sexual minorities.
- Tolerance.org at http://www.tolerance.org is a project created by the Southern Poverty Law Center and is available to educators who might be interested in antibias issues and educational materials.

Precautions and Possible Pitfalls

It should come as no surprise that specific site and community politics exist in all schools. When introducing new resources to the library, it is important that the administration supports the process. The last thing administrators want is to find out from an angry parent what is going on in the library. Libraries historically have been targets for censorship, and sexual orientation materials are often targets.

Sources

Jones, J. (2004). Beyond the straight and narrow: Libraries can give gay teens the support they need. *School Library Journal, 50*(5), 45.

Swartz, P. C. (2003). Bridging multicultural education: Bringing sexual orientation into the children's and young adult literature classrooms. *Radical Teacher, 66,* 11–16.

STRATEGY 37: Explore curriculum that includes minority sexual identity and sexuality.

What the Research Says

Swartz (2003) examines the issues surrounding curricular choices as they concern sexuality. Swartz argues for a more inclusive range of curricular materials related to sexual orientation. The author supports a proactive effort to include positive sexual minority themes in reading, writing, and talking in the classroom. The hope is that prejudices and stereotypes can be examined. Through inclusion, schools can then be made safer places for differences. For many students struggling with their sexual identity, school is a painful place. Homophobia is usually the last oppression to be mentioned, the last to be taken seriously, and is usually the last to go. Too few states and school districts attempt to diffuse the prejudices that are apparent in schools and the greater culture.

Sexual minorities are frequently misunderstood and many times only presented as a gay, white, and male. Tolerance for sexual minorities varies throughout the many cultures represented in diverse classrooms. It is unacceptable to deprive children of credible information about the range of diverse sexuality; about human social diversity; and about the power relationships within families, schools, religions, and society in general.

Swartz (2003) stresses that including curricular materials that feature themes and information about diverse sexual orientation is not to introduce alternative sexual practices. It is to open a dialogue about diverse lifestyles that exist in community and culture. Students can explore ways sexual categories are created, who is included and excluded, and how they are treated. They can explore the constructions of gender, sexuality, boundaries, and how sexism, heterosexism, and homophobia work together to constrain acceptable lifestyles and to punish transgression.

Swartz (2003) suggests a number of different media to be considered for curriculum inclusion and discusses the roles the media can play making school environments more tolerant of difference. Specific books and films are discussed for their merit in providing useful strategies in approaching sensitive issues about sexual orientation and bias.

Classroom Applications

The curricular goal should be to portray lesbians, gays, transgender youth, and bisexuals matter-of-factly, using neutral language to describe sexual minorities, and identifying lesbians and gays of accomplishment. The Web sites on the next page were selected to provide resources that could be directly considered for curriculum or the construction of curriculum. The curricular goal is not to specifically target sexual orientation issues, but to provide instruction that includes a realistic and balanced view of sexual minorities and their lives and roles in U.S. society.

These sites provide practical and useful resources. While not a comprehensive list, most sites offer many links to other sites that can also be explored.

The Safe School Coalition at http://www.safeschoolscoalition.org/RG-teachers_highschool.html

National Association of School Psychologists at http://www.nasponline.org/advocacy/resource.html

New Jersey Lesbian and Gay Coalition at http://www.njlgc.org/publications/youth_guide/edures.html

Planned Parenthood of Connecticut at http://www.ppct.org/education/curr/tackling/tackling-toc.htm

Harvard Educational Review at http://gseweb.harvard.edu/~hepg/sum96.html#pisha

The Gay, Lesbian and Straight Education Network (GLSEN) at http://www.glsen.org/cgi-bin/io wa/all/about/index.html (Check out their "Booklink" pages.)

It is interesting to note that while many Internet sites offer many ways to include diverse curriculum, in this mix there are also examples of groups that want to exclude books and other media in curriculum because of their sexual orientation content. While we have shown great gains in including ethnic and racial minority experiences in curricula, the same is not true for curricula that include the experiences of gay, lesbian, bisexual, transgender, or intersex students. If the goal is to establish fair, unbiased, balanced inclusion and representations of diverse groups in society, teachers need to create a safe place for difference.

Precautions and Possible Pitfalls

Ideally all teachers will strive to create a classroom climate that welcomes thoughtful discussion of diversity and sensitive treatment of concerns about sexual orientations. It can deepen students' understanding about identities and oppression, which, in the context of an ethnic literature curriculum, can help students develop a deeper understanding of the common ground that oppressed groups divided by difference share. When teachers make significant changes in their curriculum, they should ensure that the administration is aware of those changes and supports their efforts.

Source

Swartz, P. C. (2003). Bridging multicultural education: Bringing sexual orientation into the children's and young adult literature classrooms. *Radical Teacher*, 66, 11–16.

STRATEGY 38: *Weigh the issues of choosing to remain closeted versus coming out within educational settings.*

What the Research Says

This strategy focuses on current research relating to individuals and their decisions to self-identify publicly as a sexual minority or to remain closeted. The research considered the limitations as well as the possibilities that may surface when coming out becomes part of the educational environment. It also considers how teachers and students might benefit from being mindful of the moral, political, and pedagogical concerns that influence educational discourse and interactions.

To clarify definitions for discussion, we define *closeted* as the experience of living without disclosing one's sexual orientation or gender identity (also referred to as *being in the closet*) and *coming out* as becoming aware of one's sexual orientation or gender identity and beginning to disclose it to others. A person may be selectively *out* in some situations or to certain people without generally disclosing his or her sexual orientation or gender identity. Coming out is a process that has a temporal component that varies with the individual.

Classroom Applications

Such clean and neat definitions, like those discussed in the previous section, can overlook the difficulties relating to interfacing the sexual and educational environments. Both teachers and students who are identified as nonheterosexual face periods of self-negotiation and renegotiation of their sexual identity.

Early academic discourse tackling issues regarding sexuality and emphasizing coming out (Griffin, 1992; Harbeck, 1992) were based on the idea that coming out was empowering and valuable. This focus centered on the idea that the most effective way to change homophobic attitudes was through one-on-one personal contact. Coming out was seen as a prime strategy in reducing oppression and acts of prejudice against sexual minorities. It was also seen as a strategy to increase the psychological health of those engaged in the act of coming out. Further, teachers were encouraged to turn their identity into an element within pedagogy. Social science and English classes seemed the like the most obvious venues.

As a consequence, the politics around coming out can place people who are sexual minorities who do not come out in the position of being perceived as abdicating their responsibility, being disempowered, or ashamed of their gayness. They may be viewed as having not yet proved themselves by being honest and open.

Telford's (2003) study of young gay British university students points to the problems people encounter in efforts to come out when they enter the university environment. Drawing on interviews, Telford highlighted the way sexual identity can become suppressed by pressures from family and peer groups. Some students chose to remain closeted because of

- Fear of the withdrawal of financial support or limited access to education
- Bias within a person's racial or ethnic background and peers
- Bias within a family's religious affiliation
- Threats to the individual's or family's status within their profession or personal affiliations
- Real or perceived threats to nonheterosexuals in some educational environments

All these complications and more conspire to work against a young person's sincere desire to come out, and they can complicate his or her personal negotiation within the in/out self-identity. Ultimately, coming out is an individual and highly personal decision. Many of these factors far outweigh an individual's desire to openly assert his or her sexual identity. The problem is a political stance that does not present moral or ethical alternatives to coming out.

Whether a student or teacher, the value of taking a thoughtful and complex view of how coming out or staying closeted is connected to moral, psychological, sociological, political, and instructional environments is significant. The process of coming out or remaining closeted is far from being standardized and is constructed differently for every individual.

Precautions and Possible Pitfalls

Teachers need to ensure that they are very confident of the reactions they will receive for coming out. Special consideration needs to be given to the political climate in a given school district or community. Some communities are equipped with a variety of support resources, whereas others are not ready to embrace sexual diversity.

Sources

Griffin, P. (1992). From hiding out to coming out: Empowering lesbian and gay educators. In K. Harbeck (Ed.), *Coming out of the classroom closet* (pp. 167–196). New York: Harrington Park Press.

Harbeck, K. (1992). *Coming out of the classroom closet.* New York: Harrington Park Press.

Rasmussen, M. L. (2004). The problem of coming out. *Theory and Practice*, 43(2), 144–150.

Telford, D. (2003). The university challenge: Transition to university. In D. Epstein, S. O'Flynn, & D. Telford (Eds.), *Silenced sexualities in schools and universities* (pp. 121–140). Stoke on Trent, Staffordshire, England: Trentham Books.

 STRATEGY 39: Consider the effect of teachers coming out.

What the Research Says

 For teachers coming out, there are many questions to answer on how they will manage their various identities within and around school settings. In his article, "Teaching as a Gay Man," Silin (1999) explores the following questions:

- What goals do we achieve when we open our lives for public inspection?
- What risks do we take?
- How is pedagogy changed when we dismantle the wall between our private and professional experience?

Coming out can occur informally through the way body language and personal attributes are read by students or through purposeful dialogue. Some are perceived as nonheterosexual no matter what is said or not said. There is a distinction made between teachers who are outed because of the tone of their voice or body language and teachers who are outed because of their speech content.

Silin feels that by coming out he encourages authentic voices and dialogue with his students and classes. He uses his outings as an instructional device in examining a number of themes and topics. Questions arise about whether the same goals could be realized using other instructional materials. Questions also arise in regard to the temporal nature of one's sexual identity and whether freezing it by outing could cause problems if and when it changes. For less worldly or thoughtful students, it can also define the teacher as standing for an entire group and perpetuate stereotypes. There is also a question about which disciplines are the most appropriate for using teacher sexual identity. Some classes seem more appropriate than others. Therefore, some see coming out in the classroom as pedagogically risky, possibly self-serving, and a distraction to learning. Finally, it appears in the research that coming out is neither good nor bad. Ultimately, the pedagogical consequences of coming out will vary and depend on the individual teachers, the school, community, parents, and student body.

Classroom Applications

There are valid arguments for and against a teacher coming out. Whether grappling with sexual identity and sexual orientation issues in more traditional instructional materials or with personal contact and discourse with an outed teacher, there are no right answers.

Teachers may find an advantage in creating a supportive setting for sharing personal information. Consider a small group setting with an understanding of confidentiality as a starting point. As comfort levels increase and support is demonstrated, teachers can expand their personal disclosure.

Precautions and Possible Pitfalls

Arguments compelling people to come out often fail to consider race. In urban settings with diverse ethnic and racial groups, educators need to recognize that each culture presents different factors and elements regarding sexual orientation, and teachers' personal experiences and knowledge may not prepare them to deal with specific group values and norms. Be careful not to stereotype strategies and potential solutions. Take the time to learn what is needed to be effective. In some settings an outed teacher may not be held in the same light as in another. Some teachers, through force of personality and a positive teaching track record, will be seen differently than others.

Source

Silin, J. G. (1999). Teaching as a gay man: Pedagogical resistance or public spectacle? *GLQ: A Journal of Lesbian and Gay Studies, 5*(1), 95–106.

STRATEGY 40: *Be aware of the diverse and complex path that gay males undertake in self-defining themselves as gay.*

What the Research Says

The overall findings suggest that gay men experience varying degrees of internal and external conflict before self-identifying (coming out) as gay. The term *coming out* is described as the gap between the time individuals first report awareness of same-sex attraction and the time they fully self-identify as gay.

Discovering one's sexual identity is an important and sometimes confusing part of human development. Lesbian, gay, bisexual, or transgender youth can begin to feel differently from their peers as early as kindergarten, although there is no sexual concept accompanying those feelings. Full assumption of one's sexual identity usually occurs around the age of 15 or 16 years, but this varies by individual as does the degree of uncertainty about self-concept.

In this research, 16 gay men and 1 male adolescent were interviewed. One individual was identified as a "drag queen" and another as a "leatherman." Two participants, who were HIV positive, died before they could review their stories. All participants came from the Edmonton and Calgary areas of Canada and completed a clinical sexual orientation questionnaire. Each participant self-identified as gay and reported having a positive gay identity. All indicated they had a very strong homosexual inclination based on sexual fantasies, behavior, affect, and preference for males.

Literature searches suggest a six-year gap between a first-reported awareness of same-sex attraction—and self-identification as gay, lesbian, or bisexual—and disclosure to others. Some literature suggests that this gap is getting smaller from an 8- to 10-year gap reported in earlier research. What was missing from this research was a detailed look at what happens during this germination period.

The conflicts described during this gap period were characterized as struggles between the catalysts that inform gay boys and men they are gay and hindrances that serve to suppress these affirming messages. The research went on to discuss specific catalysts, hindrances, and their consequences. Conflicts in these factors lead to increased risks of suicide attempts, substance abuse problems, and other related stresses.

One research participant recalls,

I remember going to the school counselor and telling her "I think I am gay," and being told that it was a phase. That's the thing you hear a lot. That it's a phase and you're too young to know. I said, "No, I'm not too young to know, I know," and she said, "Well," and then I kind of . . . I haven't really thought about the process that I went through to be who I am, really." (David, age 15) (Alderson & Jevane, 2003)

David's comments illustrate a number of problems heterosexual educators have when dealing with sexual minorities. Some heterosexuals may have attitudes and beliefs that view heterosexuality as the norm and sexual minorities as immoral, inferior, sinful, or perverted. Others, who may or may not exhibit these biases, suffer from ignorance, misinformation, and lack of knowledge regarding sexual minorities. In other cases, bias can be subtle. For example, not mentioning same-sex couples when discussing relationships, excluding alternative student relationships from everyday discourse, or seeing puberty as only a heterosexual experience can exclude certain students. Still others prefer the code-of-silence strategy. They claim they don't have a problem with gay people but internally they don't understand gay behavior and wonder about demonstrative behavior in public.

Statistics vary within the research, but Hillier and Rosenthal (2001) and Philipp (1999) indicate approximately 10 percent of men are gay and 5 percent of women are lesbian. With all the coming-of-age issues that educational professionals deal with, no one would accept ignoring issues affecting 10 percent of students with nonheterosexual sexual orientations.

Alderson and Jevane's (2003) research identifies some catalysts that begin to affirm a young person's gay sexual orientation:

- Feeling different: Most gay males feel different from an early age. Feeling different is described as being aware of a same-sex attraction at an early age or displaying cross-gender interests from a young age.
- Sexual fantasies and dreams: The sexual fantasies and dreams of gay males often draw attention to homoeroticism. One subject listed this as the predominant factor in his self-definition as gay.
- Sexual and erotic arousal and attraction: Most researchers use the Kinsey Scale to measure sexual orientation and emphasize whom subjects are most strongly attracted to as a measure.
- Incomplete or unsatisfying connections to females: Approximately half of gay men have had sexual experiences with women. Subjects in their study found something was lacking in heterosexual experiences. Either their enjoyment was compromised, or their ability to fall deeply in love was limited.
- Sexual acts: Some subjects, with inner strength and opportunity for engaging in sexual acts with other males, found their sexual experiences led them to self-identification as gay.
- Falling in love with another male: Not all gay men come to self-identity as gay through sexual experimentation. Falling in love or feeling infatuated seemed to give away what lies in the heart. Some researchers, cited in Alderson and Jevane's study, felt falling in love was the definitive criteria for thinking about and defining sexual orientation.

Alderson and Jevane (2003) also identified "hindrances" or forces that hinder or stifle awareness and coming out:

- Internal homophobia: When negative beliefs about gay people enter the minds of gay individuals, it is called internalized homophobia. Most people internalize the norms, values, customs, and ideals of the majority culture. If these are negative, internal conflicts can create barriers that gay men will need to overcome during the coming out period.

- Self-concept or self-esteem related: The desire to live in denial or run from internalized homophobia creates self-esteem problems.
- Minimization and denial: Before coming out many males minimize or deny their feelings. This can sometimes go on for years.
- Overcompensation and distraction: Researchers described half their sample group as holding back their homosexual feelings and compensating by becoming extremely productive or focused on work.
- Consequences of denial: Half the study group suffered from unhappiness and depression or feeling like an impostor or a fake. These consequences can lead to self-destructive acts.
- Heterofacsimille: This is a term the researchers used to describe gays' attempts to come across as heterosexual; or at least come across as more masculine. The subliminal message here is that it's not okay to be gay.
- External hindrances: These are the external pressures that non-gays consciously or unwittingly often marginalize or minimize gay people with. Negative cultural and society norms (religion, cultural taboos), parents in denial, peer-pressure, negative stereotypes, isolation, and rejection all contribute to hindrance factors.

These identified catalysts and hindrances serve as powerful influences in a homosexual male's struggle to self-identify and come out as gay. The researchers conclude with the caveat that each gay male's development is unique.

Classroom Applications

Educators need to appreciate the diverse and complex paths that males undertake in self-defining as gay. They also need to be aware of the negative consequences of the psychic battle that gays experience as many of the battles occur during their school years. With knowledge, Alderson and Jevane felt that therapeutic professionals have the opportunity to address the factors that influence the balance between the catalysts and the hindrances. There lies the hope in making the coming out process a less stressful path.

The work teachers do with gay youth is loaded with a wide range of potential pitfalls. There are no approved protocols or *right* answers for every situation. The boundaries of responsibility can be confusing and overlap or conflict with parents, religion, or other factors outside of the school. It would be easy for a teacher to overstep these boundaries. However, teachers can reduce the external hindrances in their classrooms by becoming more sensitive to classroom discourse and the language that students use in class and elsewhere. Teachers can also create curriculum that is sensitive to sexual orientation issues.

With regard to working with individuals, most teachers, as professionals, don't get directly involved in sexual coming-of-age issues but are sensitive to them. Teachers refer students to counselors if they suspect there are serious problems. There may be a counselor or another faculty member who is more sensitive and comfortable with sexual orientation issues. Talk to them and collaborate on a course of action. There also may be a faculty member who is perceived by the student body as more trustworthy and effective with these issues. Use them.

Precautions and Possible Pitfalls

Self-reflection is important in identifying where teachers are with being sensitive to the issues described in the research. If they feel knowledge deficient or intimidated by the subject, they should seek help in creating an accurate knowledge base in understanding these issues. By doing this, teachers may help some of their students find a smoother path to mental health and peace of mind.

Sources

Alderson, K. G., & Jevane, R. F. J. (2003). Yin and yang in mortal combat: Psychic conflict in the coming-out process of gay males. *Guidance and Counseling*, *18*(4), 28–41.

Hillier, L., & Rosenthal, D. (2001). Special issue on gay, lesbian and bisexual youth. *Journal of Adolescence*, *24*, 1–4.

Philipp, S. F. (1999). Gay and lesbian tourist at a Southern U.S.A. beach event. *Journal of Homosexuality*, *37*, 69–86.

Weiler, E. R. (2003). Legally and morally, what our gay students must be given. *Education Digest*, *69*(5), 38–43.

STRATEGY 41: Work to prevent low-level violence in schools.

What the Research Says

Duper and Meyer-Adams (2002) define and categorize what is described as low-level underlying school violence. While not violent in a physical sense, this form of violence is defined as *verbal violence* between students and student groups, and between teachers and students.

In their paper, Dupper and Meyer-Adams (2002) rely on a literature search for data and examine a number of sources that contribute to a larger picture of the effects of this sort of violence on the school climate and specific students.

Bullying is estimated to affect 15 percent to 20 percent of the U.S. student population, with verbal teasing and intimidation being the most common forms. Bullying appears to peak in middle and junior high schools (Batsche & Knoff, 1994). The impact of bullying on its victims includes loss of self-esteem and psychological isolation. Victims divert large amounts of energy that could be expended on learning to avoid harm and deal with the abuse. Bullies are five times more likely to end up in juvenile court, be convicted of crimes, and have children with aggression issues.

A survey of 1,600 white, African American, and Hispanic students in secondary schools conducted by the American Association of University Women (AAUW) (1993) finds 85 percent of girls and 76 percent of boys report experiencing some form of sexual harassment. Sexual harassment is described as nonphysical (sexual comments, jokes, gestures, looks, sexual rumors, and flashing) to physical (touching, grabbing, and pinching). The most common forms were verbal (65 percent of girls and 42 percent of boys). The results of this type of low-level violence include not wanting to go to school, not wanting to participant in class, and finding it difficult to pay attention in school.

Homophobic remarks were reported by more than 91.4 percent of 496 lesbian, gay, bisexual, or transgender youth in a study by the Gay, Lesbian and Straight Education Network in 1999. Pilkington and D'Augelli (1995) found that 22 percent of males and 29 percent of females reported having been physically hurt by another student as a result of their sexual orientation. Dupper and Meyer-Adams (2002) believe that school personnel rarely intervene when students are victimized. They also found that some guidance counselors harbored negative feelings toward these sexual orientations, and they located research that found homophobic remarks somewhat common among faculty and staff (Massachusetts Governor's Commission on Gay and Lesbian Youth, 1993). It is not surprising that this form of harassment would affect school performance.

Some teachers routinely use sarcasm, loud outbursts, threats, or ridicule to control students in their classrooms. Many times teachers spend more time relating to students on control issues than curricular issues. There is a gray area where discipline and control techniques become intimidation by adults in authority. While there is little research on the subject, Dupper and Meyer-Adams (2002) this type of communication as low-level violence.

The investigation goes on to describe how these types of low-level violence change the climate and culture of schools. They make some suggestions for change and reform and suggest a number of programs and examples of schools that have been successful in developing proactive strategies to deal with these problems.

Dupper and Meyer-Adams (2002) suggest several programs that address bullying issues and focus on developing a more positive school culture and climate. Further, they state that the Office of Juvenile Justice and Delinquency Prevention (OJJDP) has recognized the Bullying Prevention Program as one of its 10 Blueprint Programs because it has shown the ability to prevent violence. Dupper and Meyer-Adams's research found two schools in California that have been highlighted for their efforts to reduce school violence with a focus on changing school culture and climate. Oakland's Emiliano Zapata Street Academy and Clear View Elementary School in Chula Vista are cited as models well worth considering. A quick search on the Internet locates numerous references to these schools' successes in this area and descriptions of some of their programs for reducing violence.

The strengths of many of these programs are contained in the effort of school staff to get to know their students better. They also have some longer class periods, ranging from 1 to 1½ hours rather than the usual 40 to 45 minutes. Homerooms and homeroom-like settings allow teachers to interact with students beyond the instructional focus.

Classroom Applications

Every student should have the right to be spared oppression and repeated, intentional humiliation in schools. Schools must send a strong message to students and staff that all forms of low-level violence are inappropriate and adults will actively intervene in all instances. Those who fail to do so are actually promoting violence.

Because many school personnel do not acknowledge that low-level violence is a problem, it is essential that a needs assessment be conducted and that all school personnel be informed about the extent of bullying, sexual harassment, sexual orientation victimization, and psychological maltreatment students experience. When ignored, low-level violence lowers academic achievement, undermines physical and emotional well-being, and may provoke violence.

The best way to reduce low-level violence is to create a school culture and climate characterized by warmth, tolerance, and positive responses to diversity. Sensitivity to others' views, cooperative interactions among students, and teacher and school staffs that create an environment that expects and reinforces appropriate behavior contribute to that positive learning environment.

Rather than focus on the victims and perpetrators, effective interventions must happen on a variety of levels. Training and workshops can help train teachers to take leadership roles in discussions, activities, and interventions that directly target issues of low-level violence. This can then be extended to the classroom as a standard of conduct for all teachers. Grades six through eight are critical targets for proactive activities and can begin to set a positive trajectory as students move on toward high school.

Precautions and Possible Pitfalls

 Because of the lack of specific research, psychological maltreatment of students by teachers is not fully explored in the research. Needless to say, teachers need to reflect on their own communicative style. If they find that their conversations with students deal more with management and discipline and not curricular or instructional issues, they may want to examine the nature of their interactions with those students.

If teachers find they are using a loud voice, sarcasm, threats, and ridicule routinely they may want to consider looking for help. Threats and sarcasm can be effective in the short term, but they often backfire. They're difficult to defend in parent conferences, and they create a hostile work environment for both the teacher and the students.

Sources

American Association of University Women (AAUW). (1993). *Hostile hallways: AAUW survey on sexual harassment in America's schools.* Washington, DC: Author.

Batsche, G. M., & Knoff, H. M. (1994). Bullies and their victims: Understanding a pervasive problem in the schools. *School Psychology Review, 23,* 165–174.

Dupper, D. R., & Meyer-Adams, N. (2002). Low-level violence: A neglected aspect of school culture. *Urban Education, 37*(3), 350–364.

Massachusetts Governor's Commission on Gay and Lesbian Youth. (1993). *Making schools safe for gay and lesbian youth: Report of the Massachusetts governor's commission on gay and lesbian youth.* Boston: Author.

Pilkington, N. W., & D'Augelli, A. R. (1995). Victimization of lesbian, gay and bisexual youth in community settings. *Journal of Community Psychology, 23,* 34–56.

Gay, Lesbian, and Straight Education Network. (1999). *GLESN's national school climate survey: Lesbian, gay, bisexual, and transgender students and their experiences in school.* Retrieved March 18, 2005 from http://www.glsen.org/pages/sections/newsnatlnews/1999/sep/survey

5

Supporting Students Who Are Economically Disadvantaged

One of the most powerful tools for empowering individuals and communities is making certain that any individual who wants to receive a quality education can do so.

Christine Gregoire

STRATEGY 42: Teach group skills to help low-income students establish a positive and encouraging support network to increase their likelihood of attending and completing higher education.

What the Research Says

 In an analysis of the factors that lead students from low-income families not to finish college, researchers Stinebrickner and Stinebrickner (2003) isolated several key factors that contribute to the less than 11 percent completion of low-income students. The students in this study were not required to pay tuition or other expenses, so other factors linked to low-income may have adversely affected their performance at the college level. Using data taken from the administration of Berea College in Kentucky, which offers generous subsidies for tuition and housing, the researchers were able to consider the issue of high attrition of low-income students separate from the direct costs of attending college. The researchers noted three key factors from study respondents: lack of preparation because of less challenging elementary and high schools, lack of parent support and encouragement, and lack of educational instruction at home as factors in student dropout rates.

Classroom Applications

Few can argue that all students achieve more when they are supported and encouraged to perform to their potential. While many teachers take on the role of "cheerleader" for students from all income levels, students from lower-income families may need support past the time that they are involved with a specific teacher. When families are unable to provide support through ignorance or unwillingness, students can find support and encouragement from their peers. By providing opportunities for student bonding and ongoing and effective teamwork, teachers can proactively enhance students' skills in supporting each other academically.

By actively and specifically teaching the skills that are involved in effective group dynamics, teachers can contribute to student success in group situations. Some teachers in the lower grade levels approach group activities by assigning specific group roles and related responsibilities. Titles like Manager, Summarizer, Materials Manager, and Recorder clearly indicate to students that there are different aspects of group work that need to be accomplished to complete the task successfully. By rotating these roles, each student has the opportunity to experience what is involved in each part. Typically, groups will meet four times, and then the entire group will change members and move on to work with a different group. Although this is an effective practice for building community as a class, teachers should consider the advantages to letting students stay together longer to help forge strong supportive relationships. By considering students' private input regarding group formation, teachers may be able to spot positive and supportive relationships as they form and encourage their growth through lesson design and group work planning.

At higher grade levels, teachers might consider inviting teams to write a charter prior to beginning their group assignment. Common topics to include in the charter are

- *Team Skill Inventory*, which highlights areas of strength that each team member brings to the team
- *Team Goals*, which often include the specific assignment(s)
- *Potential Barriers* to achieving these goals, which often include time issues, difficulty finding information
- *Ground Rules* which address how often the team will meet, agenda, communication methods, etc.
- *Conflict Management*, which addresses potential conflicts that may arise and how the team will resolve them

After a team has outlined its charter, the communication methods are usually clear and team members are better equipped to work as a group compared to a group that just leaps into the assignment first. Again, teachers can contribute to strengthening the connection among group members by allowing the groups to continue working together for an extended series of assignments.

Precautions and Possible Pitfalls

 It is important that teachers facilitate the communication among group members, particularly if the communication process breaks down. Asking for private feedback from group members regarding the group process can serve as a positive reflection tool as well as an early warning system to alert teachers about groups that may need additional assistance.

Source

Stinebrickner, R., & Stinebrickner, T. R. (2003). Understanding educational outcomes of students from low-income families. *Journal of Human Resources*, *38*(3), 591–618.

 STRATEGY 43: *Use cooperative test review and study guides to improve student achievement.*

What the Research Says

 In keeping with the rise in use of cooperative groups, researchers Steinbrink and Jones (1993) examined the effects of using cooperative grouping techniques as a test review process for increasing the performance of lower achieving and disadvantaged students. They cite five key aspects of cooperative learning: face-to-face interaction, focus on collaborative skills, positive interdependence, monitoring academic progress, and individual accountability. They also cite several research studies conducted regarding the improved performance of students using this model and go on to specifically outline the process for teachers:

Step 1: Create a test that is clear and appropriate for the subject matter.

Step 2: Create a series of study items that correspond to the test questions. It is important to physically develop a study guide that relates to both factual and skill-related items.

Step 3: After instruction and guided practice for the unit is completed, assign students to mixed-ability cooperative groups.

Step 4: Assign group roles and ensure each student has a copy of the study guide. Have the group leader ensure that each member answers the study guide prompts and facilitates the group's efforts.

Step 5: The teacher should roam the room offering clarification and support as needed.

Step 6: Conduct a whole-class review or game (Jeopardy, Family Feud, baseball, etc.) to further support students' understanding.

More recently, researchers Webb, Farivar, and Mastergeorge (2002) focused their efforts on the examination of effective cooperative group skills and teachers' roles in that process. They found four key areas of teacher responsibility: ensuring positive group norms, structuring tasks, modeling desired behaviors, and monitoring group work.

Classroom Applications

Students' test review study skills vary greatly. While some students seem to intuit beneficial study habits, others seem to have no idea where to begin. Whole-class review sessions often tend to focus on higher achieving students whose quick and correct responses may yield a false impression that the whole class understands the material and is well-prepared for the upcoming assessment. Students who have parents who are well skilled in study techniques or the specific material are also at an advantage. Some students' parents are not school savvy and have limited educational backgrounds, placing their children at a disadvantage when it comes to studying for tests. Other factors often found in conjunction with lower income students (work to help family, care for younger siblings, crowded housing, etc.) may also inhibit students' abilities to study effectively. By actively addressing effective study habits and modeling the positive aspects of study groups for test review, teachers can make a real difference in the performance of their average and lower achieving students.

Designing study guides that are effective and useful tools for specific tests also helps teachers ensure that test materials accurately assess the material taught. In addition, study guides help communicate to students the essential elements of a particular unit. Once the groups are assigned and are using the study guide to gather appropriate information, teachers can monitor student progress and make needed adjustments rather than waiting until after a test has been given to clarify specific material.

In addition, teachers can facilitate the effective interaction of students working together for a common purpose. Higher achieving students can solidify their own understanding by explaining their knowledge to their peers. Lower achieving students have the opportunity to ask questions and receive feedback on their own understanding of the material as well as a chance to see the material presented in a slightly different format, which may facilitate their understanding. The development of social skills, which may be lacking in disadvantaged students (Steinbrink & Jones, 1993), may also be enhanced through group work.

Following cooperative group work on teacher-made study guides, whole-group review with students working as teams can cement concepts and contribute to further team bonding as students demonstrate their knowledge in a game format. Depending on the material and the grade level, teachers can implement fun activities that encourage student groups to work together while sharing their understanding of the material.

Precautions and Possible Pitfalls

It is important to remember that although cooperative groups can be very effective for test review, teachers should not rely on these groups to re-teach material that has been inadequately covered during direct instruction. Also, it should be noted that some students may benefit from individualized instruction from the teacher, particularly if missing skills or gaps are contributing to student failure. Teachers may want to consider that cooperative group review may be an effective time to pull aside a student who is struggling for some one-on-one assistance.

Sources

Steinbrink, J. E., & Jones, R. M. (1993). Cooperative test-review teams improve student achievement. *Clearing House*, *66*(5), 307–312.

Webb, N. M., Farivar, S. H., & Mastergeorge, A. M. (2002). Productive helping in cooperative groups. *Theory Into Practice, 41*(1), 13–21.

STRATEGY 44: *Encourage all students to enroll in rigorous courses, and build in the needed supports to facilitate their success.*

What the Research Says

Lawrence Gladieux, Independent Consultant to the Committee on House Education and the Workforce (2002), indicates that although much has been done to address the financial barriers to lower-income students attending college, other factors need to be considered. His data indicate that 53 percent of low-income students are prepared for college compared to 86 percent of high-income students. Using the same index, 47 percent of African American students and 53 percent of Hispanic students are prepared for college compared to 68 percent of white students. He notes that students who take algebra and geometry are more likely to enroll in college, yet only 28 states require these courses for high school graduation. Students who take more rigorous and challenging courses in high school are more likely to attend and succeed in college.

Classroom Applications

Many high schools have programs like AVID (Advancement Via Individual Determination) and Upward Bound; in addition to these, however, individual teachers can have a significant impact on their students' preparedness for higher education by crafting curricula that are rigorous yet achievable. Focusing on the "big ideas" or main concepts in-depth in a subject area has a much greater impact on a student's knowledge than a broad overview course filled with memorization of insubstantial facts. Teachers can facilitate student understanding with larger projects supported by ongoing teacher evaluation and recommendations in place of many smaller, unrelated activities. In addition, teachers can imitate college coursework by providing opportunities for student exploration and evaluation of current research in a guided process format to ensure that students understand what they are reading.

Many teachers have found success by offering smaller workshops before or after school to support students who are struggling with course concepts. Some schools offer tutoring sessions free of charge, using local college students and older high school students to support students who are struggling with their studies.

Precautions and Possible Pitfalls

In their efforts to propel all students toward higher education, it can be easy for teachers to forget that not all students want to continue with formal schooling. It is essential that teachers assist all of their students so that each individual student's dream can be achieved. For some students, this might mean locating a local vocational training center or helping them access a community college certificate program. Other students may choose to work before establishing an educational goal.

Source

Gladieux, L. (2002, July 16). *Access to higher education for low-income students.* Federal Document Clearing House (FDCH) Congressional Testimony.

STRATEGY 45: *Use a variety of print materials to inspire student reading and writing.*

What the Research Says

Bracey (2001) discusses the findings of Nell Duke from Michigan State University in her research analysis of how reading is taught differently in low-socioeconomic status (SES) and high-SES first grade classrooms. The most significant difference was the variety of extended texts and activities that relate meaningfully to those texts. Although the research indicated little time difference spent on reading between the two groups, the variety of print material presented in the high-SES setting was substantial. In the high-SES classrooms, poetry, magazines, newspaper articles, and text materials were displayed prominently with student-authored work on specific topics. In the low-SES classrooms, worksheets were the primary form of print material and few examples of extended student writing occurred. Bracey also noted that low-SES school libraries had 40 percent fewer books available and seldom added to their numbers during the school year.

Classroom Applications

 Teachers need to ensure that the opportunity for reading a variety of print materials is available for their students regardless of grade level or content area. Research indicates that the more students read, the better their skills develop, and yet reading the standard classroom text often leaves students bored and unengaged, particularly if the text is outdated by student standards. Teachers need to use school librarians, the Internet, other teachers, parents, community members, and the students themselves to provide a wide range of print material.

Many local newspapers have programs for free newspaper delivery to local classrooms. Often included with these papers are curricular activities that teachers can use or adapt to their own curricular needs. Many newspaper articles are short and of higher interest to students, and will be more easily accessible for the struggling reader. Even the comics and editorial cartoons provide opportunities for students to derive meaning from printed material.

Poetry and short stories abound on the Internet and are often the perfect vehicle to introduce students to the elements of fiction in their own writing. Rhyme, rhythm, plot development, and characterization can all be addressed in context and act as a springboard for students as emerging authors.

Although worksheets may have their place in reinforcing rote memory skills, teachers would be wise to avoid relying on them as their number one way of infusing print material in their students' school day. Worksheets should be used as reinforcement rather than core curriculum. By providing a variety of print material, teachers can provide the opportunity for students to explore extended texts in meaningful ways.

Precautions and Possible Pitfalls

It is important that teachers remain mindful of school and district policy regarding materials that can be used in the classroom. Some districts allow anything and others have strict guidelines. Some districts restrict what material teachers can present to whole classes but allow students to read a broader range of content if they are reading independently. It is very important that teachers make themselves aware of these policies prior to introducing controversial materials to their classrooms. Teachers should screen the materials they bring to the classroom to ensure they are appropriate for the students and the curriculum.

Source

Bracey, G. W. (2001). Does higher tech require higher skills? *Phi Delta Kappan, 82*(9), 715–717.

STRATEGY 46: *Explore the effects of pacing on student learning when working with low-income students.*

What the Research Says

Researcher Hoadley (2003) examines the issue of instructional pacing or rate of transmission as it differs in two South African schools. The first school serves a low-income population and the second serves a middle-class population. Through extended observation and interview, Hoadley suggests that there is a significant difference in the pacing of instruction between the two settings. In the lower-income school, the teacher permits a slower pace so that all students may complete the assigned material. This practice often results in a great deal of wait time for those students who complete the work more quickly than their peers. In contrast, the teacher in the higher-income school uses a faster pace and provides a variety of differentiated activities to allow for the range of student abilities. Hoadley suggests that these differences in pacing may result from the individual teachers and their beliefs about education and their students. She indicates there are many differences between the two teachers and their perspectives. For instance, although the teacher in the lower-income school believes that parents are an important part of a child's education, there is little parent expectation and little parent involvement. In the higher-income school, the teacher actively involves parents in the educational process.

Classroom Applications

Teachers need to evaluate their beliefs about education and their students. With those beliefs in mind, teachers need to make the connection from their beliefs to their teaching practices. Pacing is one example of an aspect of instruction that is largely a teacher-controlled issue. Teachers need to evaluate their current pacing practices and the effects on student learning. If students have large amounts of unstructured time while they wait for others to catch up, teachers need to provide either differentiated instruction or alternate activities that provide for the differences in student abilities. Teachers may also want to consider the use of small-group instruction to address the needs of all students with varied abilities.

Teachers should be encouraged to explore different pacing practices and solicit student input along with their own observations to determine the most effective pacing for a group of students. Teachers should also be aware that slowing the pace of instruction should not be the first change made when the material becomes more complex. Often effective scaffolding or embedded instruction will lead to better learning outcomes than simply slowing the pace of instruction.

Precautions and Possible Pitfalls

 It is essential that teachers do not consider that a slower pace is required for students with lower abilities. A more appropriate instructional activity may prove to be a more effective intervention. It is also critical that teachers don't mistake issues in classroom management for pacing difficulties. Although inadequate pacing may lead to unstructured time that results in behavior concerns, teachers should address management issues directly and not adjust their pacing as a first response.

Source

Hoadley, U. (2003). Time to learn: Pacing and the external framing of teachers' work. *Journal of Education for Teaching*, 29(3), 265–288.

STRATEGY 47: *Teach self-regulation and attention-sustaining skills to help students improve their performance.*

What the Research Says

 Researchers Howse, Lange, Farran, and Boyles (2003) conducted a study of 127 primary grade students (85 students economically at risk and 42 not at risk) to examine the effects of motivation and self-regulation on lower-income students and their academic performance. The researchers determined that although motivation is commonly believed to be a significant difference between lower-income and higher-income students, they noted little difference between the two groups of students.

The real difference, indicated by the research (Howse et al., 2003), was the students' abilities to focus their attention to the task at hand. Lower-income students had a 30 percent rate of distractibility, which researchers believe may account for their lower scholastic performance over time.

> Because improvements in children's attention-regulation may produce lasting improvements in reading processes, teachers must organize their classrooms in ways that encourage the early use of self-regulatory strategies and illustrate for young children how to engage in task activities in deliberate, planned, and strategic ways. (Howse et al., p. 173)

Classroom Applications

Teachers need to actively and concretely address the issue of self-regulation and attention-sustaining skills, particularly when teaching students from lower-income backgrounds. Less time should be spent on building motivation as an extrinsic element, and more time should be spent on isolating the specific skills needed for academic success. Teachers can address this skill development in a variety of ways.

To illustrate basic self-regulation skills, teachers may find it beneficial to have students use a journal or log to indicate what is required for a specific assignment (e.g., draw a picture of an animal, and write a four-line poem about the animal). When the students begin the activity, teachers can help them to determine which part of the assignment to tackle first (some may choose to draw first, others may want to include parts of their poem in their illustration). To help establish the planning aspect of task completion, teachers may want to require that the assignment be completed in stages and have the students determine those stages (e.g., students may visit the school library to locate a picture of the animal, then begin the drawing or read two animal poems before composing their own original poem). When the assignment is complete, students make an appropriate notation in their journal or log. At this point, the teacher may find it beneficial to lead the students through a reflection process on the activity. In small groups, with a partner or through journaling, students can use their metacognitive skills to reflect on the assignment and make the needed adjustments for the next task.

Precautions and Possible Pitfalls

Although all students will benefit from direct instruction on planning and attention-sustaining techniques, teachers should be careful not to ignore the special needs of students with attention deficit disorder (ADD). Students with ADD also benefit from direct skill instruction but may require additional supports from teachers on an individual basis. Teachers should refer to the students' Individualized Education Programs (IEPs) for specifics on modifications or accommodations that may be required.

Source

Howse, R. B., Lange, G., Farran, D. C., & Boyles, C. D. (2003). Motivation and self-regulation as predictors of achievement in economically disadvantaged young children. *Journal of Experimental Education, 71*(2), 151–175.

STRATEGY 48: *Explore team teaching to address the needs of economically disadvantaged students.*

What the Research Says

Seven years ago, a Dallas school restructured to create a team-based model to address the needs of their student population, 86 percent of whom qualify for free/reduced federal food programs (Minnett, 2003). Each classroom team is composed of two teachers who plan, teach, and reflect together all day. Sharing a common student population, their discussions are specific and solution centered. The basic teacher team also works closely with an extended team of counselors, administrators, and parents to collaboratively address the needs of all students. Shared reflection is a key element to the team approach. Being able to examine their own practices and invite the perspectives of other team members is essential to the ongoing growth desired. Teacher teams also provide inservice to other teacher teams to share areas of expertise.

Minnett (2003) determined that the hallmark of excellent teaming was the seamless interactions between the two teachers as the result of planning. Each team meets regularly and plans the entire curriculum together. Each teacher is an active part of each lesson and can at any moment take over the lesson should an individual student need assistance from the other teacher. Behavior is seldom an issue as one teacher can address the behavior while the other continues the lesson.

Classroom Applications

Although few schools enjoy the luxury of two teachers in each classroom, there are many aspects of teaming that can be incorporated to help meet the needs of economically disadvantaged students. One of the easiest and most productive strategies is to plan curriculum as a team. Working with other teachers helps teachers refine their ideas and ensures that standards are met while creative and high interest approaches are developed. Teachers responsible for the same grade levels will find it beneficial to work together to develop lesson plans that are comprehensive yet flexible enough to incorporate each individual teacher's style. The key with team planning is to ensure regular planning sessions that are focused and productive. It is also vital that subsequent planning sessions include a time for reflection and discussion regarding previous planning.

Team planning isn't limited to grade levels; some teachers find it valuable to work with higher- and lower-grade teachers (vertical teaming) to facilitate articulation and consistency for the students. Having a constant set of rules and requirements can help ease a student's transition from grade to grade. In addition, vertical teaming allows for discussion of a student's development over time. This sort of communication can be instrumental in identifying areas of potential difficulty and/or disability.

Some teachers group their students for subject-specific teaming lessons. Two teachers and their two classes may gather in a multipurpose room, library, or outside to focus on a specific science activity or guest speaker. Many teachers at the elementary level find combining classes— this could be two classes from the same grade level or from two different grade levels—for physical education helps create a higher quality experience for both groups of children. Still other teachers find that cross-age teaming can benefit students in the lower and upper grades by facilitating a "buddy" experience.

Precautions and Possible Pitfalls

 It is important that teachers do not underestimate the skills needed to work effectively as a team. Honesty and respect are the foundation for positive communication among team members. Volunteering to be part of a team is more likely to yield positive results than being forced to team as part of an administrative decision. Teams that develop out of or into work-related friendships are the most effective for teachers and students alike.

Source

Minnett, A. M. (2003). Collaboration and shared reflections in the classroom. *Teachers & Teaching, 9*(3), 279–286.

 STRATEGY 49: Mentor economically disadvantaged students to improve their aspirations.

What the Research Says

Based on previous research indicating that mentoring is an effective way to promote the success of students who are economically disadvantaged, Jongyeun (1999) included 130 students in a study to examine the process and effect of mentoring. The mentors in this study were required to make a one-year commitment and spend at least two hours a month at the school. The students were specifically taught business etiquette and manners to raise their comfort level in meeting with their mentors. In addition, the school created a liaison position to help facilitate the interactions between the students and their mentors.

Results after one year of mentoring indicated a significant increase in student aspirations. Coupled with previous findings that students with long-term goals and aspirations are more successful than students with short-range or limited goals, this aspect of mentoring becomes very powerful. Students need to be encouraged to become aware of possible educational and career options and learn how to set appropriate goals to reach them. Mentoring can have long-lasting effects. According to Jongyeun, " . . . the visions students hold of their future give meaning to school subjects related to their visions, resulting in improved academic achievement, self-concept, attitude toward school, and attendance rates, while decreasing disciplinary and behavior problems."

Classroom Applications

 Many students who are economically disadvantaged may lack role models for higher education and career awareness options. By mentoring these students personally or acting as a liaison between students and community members who are willing to serve as mentors, teachers can greatly improve their students' goal-setting abilities and increase their future aspirations.

Mentoring should not be reserved just for high school students. This research indicates that students as young as fourth grade benefit from interaction with a mentor. Mentors have the opportunity to create positive one-on-one relationships with students. Mentors can facilitate the exploration of education and career options, help develop working knowledge and skills to ease fears, and increase confidence.

Teachers may find it beneficial to begin slowly by identifying one or two economically disadvantaged students who would be interested in meeting with a mentor. After determining the students' areas of general interest, the teacher can locate community members who have experience and expertise in those areas. The first meeting between mentor and student should be structured so that each party has a chance to learn about the other. Teachers may want to provide a written agenda to guide the interaction, and often these first meetings can include the teacher as a facilitator. After the relationship has been established, teachers can then help facilitate the ongoing relationship by keeping the lines of communication open.

Precautions and Possible Pitfalls

Teachers need to be careful not to try to implement a mentoring program with too many students at the beginning. This is particularly true if the teacher chooses to mentor a student personally. Working with one student creates a special and positive relationship; working with more can diminish the positive effects and become a negative drain on the mentor.

Source

Jongyeun, L. (1999). The positive effects of mentoring economically disadvantaged students. *Professional School Counseling, 2*(3), 172–179.

STRATEGY 50: *Make academic success the first priority for economically disadvantaged students.*

What the Research Says

In a research study examining the link between school culture and effective schools, Gaziel (1997) surveyed 20 schools in Israel. Ten of the schools were rated as average and 10 were rated as highly effective, based on student performance. Gaziel determined that the differences between the two groups could be accounted for largely as a result of school culture factors. Interestingly, the research determined that the highest priority at the highly effective schools was academic achievement. The highest priority at the average schools was orderliness. The researcher noted that teachers in the average schools working with disadvantaged students believed that academic success of the students could not be achieved before order was established. Gaziel goes on to conclude

> . . . to be effective in a disadvantaged environment, where education is less highly valued, a school must have a school culture that, first, values academic achievement; second, values continuous school improvement and teamwork; and, only then, values the creation of an orderly environment. Although orderliness is important in schools, when it becomes the sole important norm, it prevents other norms from being expressed within the school. (p. 319)

Classroom Applications

School culture can be a difficult thing to define, and needed changes in school culture most effectively begin at the ground level. While administrators may be concerned about test scores and minimizing conflict on school campuses, teachers have the opportunity to set the tone for their classrooms with the way they approach instruction. There is no question that some orderliness is essential to be able to effectively deliver instruction, but teachers need to place the greatest emphasis on academic growth and achievement in their classrooms. This is particularly important for students who are economically disadvantaged and may not have school success and higher education on their own priority list.

Teachers can demonstrate their own commitment to academic growth and success through simple techniques like weighting their grading for content with less weight on structure and format. Allow students to correct their work and resubmit it for partial or extra credit. Focus on application of higher-level thinking skills, and encourage students to take pride in their own and each other's academic successes. Share personal experiences regarding higher-level education and the positive difference it can make. Encourage students to articulate and track their personal academic goals.

Precautions and Possible Pitfalls

 Changing school culture takes time and effort, but choosing to emphasize academic success over an orderly environment does not mean that the quest for order is abandoned. Teachers who create sound processes for classroom procedures and who take the time to teach those procedures concretely often find they have more time to devote to instruction.

Source

Gaziel, H. H. (1997). Impact of school culture on effectiveness of secondary schools with disadvantaged students. *Journal of Educational Research, 90*(5), 310–319.

 STRATEGY 51: Use a variety of assessments to identify gifted students from under-represented groups, particularly economically disadvantaged students.

What the Research Says

Historically there has been ample research to support the fact that students from minority groups and lower income settings (inner-city and rural) are under-represented in gifted programs (Passow & Frasier, 1996). There are a variety of explanations for this disparity, but the primary reason seems to be the limited view that determines giftedness. Often entrance to gifted programs is based on academic performance on tests and the ability to perform in English. This practice artificially limits some students' performance and restricts their access.

Researchers Passow and Frasier (1996) suggest that broader and more dynamic views need to be used to identify students. They cite the theories of Gardner's Multiple Intelligences, Sternberg's Triarchic Theory, Renzulli's Talent Pool, and others as starting points for enlarging the traditional perspective of what talent really is. They go on to propose that teachers adapt current assessments to reflect cultural differences and include more authentic assessment instruments whenever possible. In addition, teachers need to provide a challenging curriculum that stimulates students to demonstrate their giftedness.

Classroom Applications

Many teachers strive to meet the diverse needs of their students through multimodal instruction, and, although offering a variety of instructional approaches is a good starting point, the effort also needs to be made to allow students to express their learning in a variety of modalities. This becomes particularly important when it comes to identifying students for advancement opportunities. The student who has had the opportunity to present his or her understanding of literature through an art project may be a good candidate for a higher-level or Advanced Placement art class. Often students who lack advanced skills in math and English assume they are not scholastically talented and so may fail to recognize their own giftedness as having value.

By offering a variety of opportunities for students to demonstrate their skills and by encouraging student choice in assessment medium, teachers can foster personal growth and self-awareness. In addition, these assessments can be included in the analysis of placement for a student in the honors, gifted, or advanced track.

In addition to a student's individual talents, teachers should make an effort to learn about cultural demonstrations of student ability. Certain kinds of dancing, singing, and ritual may well be a viable assessment of a student's ability if the teacher has made the effort to learn about the specifics for an individual student.

Precautions and Possible Pitfalls

Many schools today offer open access to Advanced Placement and honors classes. Teachers should be careful not to leave it at that. Equal access does not mean equal success; students who may exhibit their talents untraditionally or those who don't have a history of advanced classes may need ongoing support with academic skills and time management to be successful in higher-level classes.

Source

Passow, A. H., & Frasier, M. M. (1996). Toward improving identification of talent potential among minority and disadvantaged students. *Roeper Review, 18*(3), 198–203.

STRATEGY 52: Support equal access to extracurricular activities to promote student connectedness.

What the Research Says

In a study by Brown and Evans (2002), students who reported higher levels of involvement in extracurricular activities also reported higher levels of school connections. This was found to be particularly true among Hispanic, African, and European Americans. Participation in sports seemed to cut across ethnic categories and had similar attraction to all ethnic groups, whereas other extracurricular categories did not reflect the same diversity and appeal as sports.

Most teachers have an intuitive sense that student participation in extracurricular activities has some positive connection to success in school. Therefore a student's sense of connection can be used as a predictor of success and behavior both inside and outside the classroom setting. While this study focused on the relationship between participation in both school-related and outside of school extracurricular activities and a sense of school connection, it also went further. It examined differences in participation rates for different activities and also broke down ethnicity as an element in participation. The results were discussed in terms of creating less-restricted pathways and more opportunities for diverse students.

Data were taken from students in two Northern California–San Francisco East Bay school districts. Targeted schools serviced students from inner-city, urban, and suburban neighborhoods. They also varied in socioeconomic status, ranging from 5 percent to more than 90 percent of their students coming from families who receive aid from the Temporary Assistance for Needy Families program. The sample group of 1,739 secondary students represented a mix of students in these ethnic categories: Hispanic American, 18 percent; African American, 17 percent; European American, 22 percent; Asian American, 15 percent; Pacific Islander, 4 percent; mixed ethnicity/other, 22 percent; and Native American, 3 percent.

Classroom Applications

The availability of extracurricular activities does not ensure equal access for all students. The current values, standards, and expectations in school settings, including extracurricular activities, reflect the dominant European American majority student population. Other student populations may feel isolated or lack support regarding inclusion in such activities. While inclusion in extracurricular activities may foster positive peer group interaction and a sense of belonging, those most at risk may experience a very different path to participation. Fees, transportation problems, lack of parental support or family obligations, grade point average requirements, or lack of peer support can all create an uneven playing field for some student groups. To add to the problem, there are issues of individual skill, expertise, talent, popularity, or student-body status that contribute to decisions. Many of these activities are very competitive. Marginalized groups are often the ones that could benefit the most from participation, yet their road to participation is often hardest. These issues may be more apparent for out-of-school extracurricular activities as the responsibility shifts more from school to the home in some low-income communities.

All these potential barriers, combined with different participation rates in certain ethnic groups, suggest that teachers, administrators, schools, parents, and communities need to do a better job of leveling the playing field. They need to make the programs more inclusive and attractive to all students.

Another key finding from the Brown and Evan research was the connection between non–school-sponsored afterschool programs and their relationship to school connection. The research found that they were significantly related to school success and the avoidance of risky adolescent behavior. Schools can find ways to acknowledge and compliment student participation in these activities. Talent nights, exhibitions, and art shows give students the opportunity to demonstrate skills, talent, or mastery in their specific activity. These events should not be limited to school-sponsored activities. Teachers can make it a point to become familiar with and acknowledge individual students involved in these activities outside the school setting.

As urban communities and educational settings become more diverse, schools can find ways to involve more students and eliminate the barriers identified that inhibit students from diverse student populations. If schools are looking for strategies to create a greater sense of student and community ownership and connection to the school, extracurricular programs are a great place to focus effort. Schools can find methods to address barriers to family and community involvement in these programs.

Finally, extracurricular activities often reflect the character and style of individual teachers and mentors. It is up to teachers to facilitate and reach out to all students, not just the easy participants. The elimination of barriers begins with involvement of the coaches, mentors, and directors of these programs.

Precautions and Potential Pitfalls

 Teachers who are not involved directly in extracurricular activities can still impact a student's life by recognizing his or her individual skills or interest in particular activities. Acknowledgement and encouragement of the efforts of the student can make a difference. Many times it will take more than a one-time effort to move a student to participate. A positive suggestion to other teachers, family, or peers can help. Encourage a coach or activity director to make a student contact. It may take some persistence to find success.

Source

Brown, R., & Evans, W. P. (2002). Extracurricular activity and ethnicity: Creating greater school connection among diverse student populations. *Urban Education*, *37*(1), 41–58.

STRATEGY 53: *Use popular films featuring urban classrooms as starting points for reflection and critical analysis.*

What the Research Says

Urban minority schools and communities have been a frequent source of subject matter for Hollywood films. For the nonurban public and many new or preservice educators, many of these movies have reinforced naïve beliefs about teaching and learning by featuring classrooms where students are featured in cliché teacher-student relationships. The Grant (2002) study looks at three popular films: *Dangerous Minds*, *Stand and Deliver*, and *187*. Teachers in these movies are defined by their personal involvement with students in the context of rescuing them from the pathology of their communities and homes. The researcher finds these movies, while containing some bits of truth about teaching and learning, also confirm and reflect many of the cliché myths or distorted concepts that teachers have about urban classrooms and teacher-student relationships. While she points out many fallacies in all three movies, her main thread of concern is the conflict between a student-centered constructionist approach to teaching and the teacher-centered and focused approach found in these three films.

In addition, professional relationships, parent relationships, and cultural differences are misrepresented, according to the researcher. She points out that in these films it is much easier to think of the classrooms' problems as a result of the incompetence of teachers rather than of other forces in the students' lives. She goes on to point out there are many forces that influence urban students, and these films exhibit little or limited understanding about what urban schools are really like. While they can be inspiring on the surface, they gloss over many serious and complex conditions and compress events in the lives of the teachers and students.

However, she feels that when examined critically, these films can provide a starting point for reflection about learning and teaching, inclusion, and urban communities.

Classroom Applications

 Teachers should watch these films (and others like them) and contrast and compare what they see with the teaching and learning philosophy they have been taught and have come to know in their professional experience. Grant (2002) offers the following question triggers for critical analysis of current and prior concepts new teachers have about urban settings:

- What exactly do urban teachers and students do in the film? What aspects of their lives are glossed over or omitted?
- What kinds of people do you see living in the urban environments of these films? What kinds of people are missing?
- What violence do you see in the films? How does this aspect of urban education compare or contrast with actual statistics and with reports in the media?
- What are the physical, social, psychological, emotional, and cognitive consequences of centuries of poverty and racism in the films? How are these issues addressed in the films?

Teachers should begin to replace their cliché beliefs and misunderstandings using critical reflection. They should help their students think about them also. Try exchanging ideas and thoughts with students and others who entered the profession with the same idealistic and caring feelings. Teachers should think about the barriers that caring parents face and are frequently overwhelmed by. What were the parents' experiences with school and what can teachers do if their view and the parents' view of the students are different? Examining these questions will help teachers develop a more realistic view of urban teaching and get beyond the Hollywood version of the urban classroom. These films can be a starting point.

Precautions and Potential Pitfalls

The transition period between being a student of education and becoming a classroom teacher is difficult. Urban settings can make this period a real test. This period puts new teachers at their greatest risk of leaving the profession. Many researchers point to preservice field experiences with seasoned teachers, students, parents, and community members as key points in discovering and internalizing the realities of the urban settings. There is a big difference between being conceptually prepared for the classroom and having real field experiences to draw on.

Source

Grant, P. A. (2002). Using popular films to challenge preservice teachers' beliefs about teaching in urban schools. *Urban Education*, 37(1), 77–95.

 STRATEGY 54: Be aware of the factors that contribute to the failure of highly competent students.

What the Research Says

 This study (Maggi, Hertzman, Kohen, & D'Angiulli, 2004) claims to be the first attempt to directly analyze the limiting factors that reduce the success rate of highly competent students between kindergarten and seventh grade because of socioeconomic indicators in a student's neighborhood. A cross-sectional analysis of the differences between highly competent kindergarten, fourth grade, and seventh grade students was used to gather data. The researchers explored the extent to which those differences are associated with neighborhood socioeconomic characteristics and social class composition.

Results support the idea that neighborhood socioeconomic status or factors are weakly connected to highly competent kindergarten students. In contrast, by grades four and seven, the proportion of highly competent children correlated strongly with neighborhood socioeconomic factors. Finally, the proportion of students at risk was strongly and increasingly connected with the proportion of highly competent children in kindergarten and in grades four and seven.

Maggi et al. (2004) collected data from schools in the Vancouver School District. Data were used to investigate the association of neighborhood socioeconomic characteristics, classroom composition, and early childhood cognitive and language development with school performance in reading and math at the targeted grade levels. Eighty-eight schools were surveyed, and data from various research instruments came from roughly 97 percent of all kindergarten students in Vancouver. This was cross-referenced with neighborhood socioeconomic indicators to predict the proportion of highly competent students with above-average competencies and their school performance in kindergarten and grades four and seven.

The study offers a number of potential explanations for why highly competent children develop a pattern of not reaching their full learning potential.

Classroom Applications

Veteran teachers probably don't need research to know that students' neighborhood and socioeconomic levels contribute to their ability to develop their learning potential. This research, however, takes the idea a step further by looking at the phenomenon over time. The general idea behind this work is that many new teachers might not be aware of the phenomenon. Once they are made aware, they can develop strategies to remedy or mitigate the phenomena. Here are the researchers' best explanations for the patterns they found:

• Highly competent students living in lower socioeconomic neighborhoods are being held back by the academic pace that tends to characterize classrooms with large numbers of children who display difficulties in learning, regardless of the style and quality of instruction. A class of 30 students from affluent neighborhoods can expect fewer children exhibiting cognitive delay and only three or four children that have any form of developmental vulnerability. In contrast, in the less affluent neighborhoods a class of 30 may expect more children who experience learning difficulties and more than 10 children with some form of learning development problems. Low-socioeconomic communities tend to concentrate vulnerable children. The pace of instruction and the rigor of instruction slow in response to this phenomenon.

• More highly qualified teachers are attracted to higher socioeconomic schools, and they are better prepared to meet the special needs of highly competent students. The effort and preparation needed to maintain an adequate learning pace and educational environment in vulnerable classrooms may lead to teacher burnout, transfer requests, and flight from the situations.

• Less-motivated teachers are more willing to stay in vulnerable classrooms and "go through the motions."

• Teachers in these highly vulnerable classrooms may fail to develop and manage the complex school-community relations. Multicultural communities present unique problems that affect parent-teacher relationships. Less "full service buy-in" by the teacher produces low-morale classrooms, possible indifference, and a slower classroom pace with reduced rigor.

In truth, all these explanations can contribute to the problem in various proportions. So how do teachers mitigate or eliminate a diverse classroom composition in which vulnerable students decrease the academic pacing experienced by students identified as highly competent? Responsible teachers who are made aware of the phenomena can begin to avoid the associated pitfalls of the situation and focus on eliminating the problem for the most vulnerable.

The focus could examine class size, teaching professional development and supervision, or better the training of teacher aides. Solutions could also center on burnout in vulnerable classrooms and possibly rotating highly motivated teachers through high burnout schools. Adding incentives for highly motivated teachers might also offer some relief.

Finally, when responsible teachers are made aware of the phenomenon, it is expected that most would work to make the adjustments necessary to reduce the impact of community factors.

Precautions and Potential Pitfalls

 Attendance boundaries change, new schools are built, and the complexion of any community can change. Haphazard or random changes to highly competent versus vulnerable student ratios and cross-active and changing demographic boundaries change the risk factors in classes. Because of these variables, it would be a mistake to stereotype any situation.

Source

Maggi, S., Hertzman, C., Kohen, D., & D'Angiulli, A. (2004). Effects of neighborhood socioeconomic characteristics and class composition on highly competent children. *The Journal of Educational Research, 98*(2), 109–114.

6

Meeting the Needs of English Language Learners

Embracing diversity is one adventure after another, opening new paths of discovery that connect an understanding to caring, listening, and sharing with others who are different than ourselves. Learning to embrace diversity begins with the attitude of transformation.

April Holland

 STRATEGY 55: *Be wary of low expectations for language minority students.*

What the Research Says

 In Tapia's (2000) study, research was conducted in Tucson, Arizona, where 25 percent of the city's 400,000 people are of Mexican descent. The city's Mexican demographic is represented by descendants of the original settlers of the city when it was controlled by Spain and later Mexico. New immigrants are primarily from the Mexican state of Sonora. Many families are considered "cross-border" families because they make frequent trips across the border for jobs, family, and many other reasons.

The goal of this study was to measure the relative weight of specific factors in shaping Mexican American students' school performance. The factors included interplay of cultural, economic, linguistic, and educational factors. Household analysis was used to illustrate how students' schooling and academic achievement were influenced by the household members' activities at home, in the community, and in the schools.

Most of the data were collected over a three-year period from 1988 to 1991. Thirty households were studied as part of a larger project; however, data were only collected from 15 households, and only 4 households were selected for in-depth studies. These households were visited between 15 and 23 times. The data collected gave clues and patterns to a study of economic and cultural survival, adaptation, and schooling practices.

The household analysis indicates that the level of family stability and the social and economic conditions of poor communities are the strongest factors affecting students' learning and academic achievement. The researcher argued that Mexican American students' learning and academic achievement will be better understood when seen in an accurate cultural and community context.

Four families investigated in Tapia's (2000) study had a total of 12 children split among them. The majority of the children were cycling through middle school and high school. Many of the parents attended school in Mexico, and none of the parents had attended college. While this research was more anecdotal in nature, some patterns did emerge that could be seen as unique for the community demographics studied. These patterns illustrate educational vulnerabilities that occur more frequently in Mexican American cultures. The study presented some student situations or snapshots typical of these Mexican American communities (Tapia, pp. 28–40) and the author's own experience:

• Family 1: This family's children were highly influenced by several residential moves during the study period. School activities and academic performance were mitigated by unsettled living conditions. The family first came across the border and lived with grandparents. The household was full of cousins and other family members. After a year, the family moved to an apartment in another school district. The parents opted to keep the children in a bilingual program and keep their former address and returned there after school. An additional move to another house did result in a move to a new school. The change in curriculum required the children to step up to a more demanding curriculum and more homework. They had become accustomed to being with friends after school and didn't adjust well to homework demands.

- Family 2: This family had three school-age children that began their schooling in Mexico and then moved to the Tucson area and into a bilingual program. While learning to read and write in English, they were also encouraged to read and write in Spanish. The students did well and the parents, although not completely understanding the curriculum, continued to help their children. One day the father became enraged over his daughter's history assignment on the United States–Mexican War. The title was "The Mythology of the Alamo." In this assignment the Mexicans were depicted in a less-than-positive light and as troublemakers. The parents felt the teachers were teaching students using stereotypes and prejudices toward minorities, and they felt this was disrespectful. All communication from the parents stopped.

- Family 3: Jose, the oldest sibling of this large family, was frequently placed in highly academic classes and played on the school's soccer team. As a junior, he became a varsity player. There were high expectations for the varsity team the following year when the team would be made up of a majority of seniors. Jose found academic success although his record of completing homework was mixed. He was part of a small group of Mexican American players that formed a core of the team. Conflicts for Jose began in his senior year when he did not return from a Christmas trip to Mexico until school league play was well under way. His family's economic situation changed between his junior and senior years. Not only did he miss his winter break obligations to his soccer team, he returned to school from his trip to Mexico two weeks past the traditional winter break, which compromised his academic standing. Rather than practice soccer, Jose was asked to watch his younger brothers and sisters after school. He was demoted to junior varsity and was forced to play with younger students who were not as skillful players. This placement lasted until grades came out in the middle of the season, when Jose became academically ineligible to play on any team. From there Jose lost all motivation for school, went to work to help support his family, and dropped out of school in his senior year. In this case, there were no calls home from any school representative, and Jose just dropped out of sight.

- Family 4: Seven people lived in the Sanchez household. Mr. Sanchez was born in Sonora, Mexico, where he completed 12 years in Mexican schools. He worked as a musician in Mexico and repaired cars in Tucson. Mrs. Sanchez completed 9 years in Mexican schools and worked in a potato chip factory. The three oldest sons were born in Sonora and ranged in age from 14 to 18 years old. The youngest two children were born in Arizona and were 4 and 12 years old. The family's household survival strategies had direct and indirect effects on the students' schooling. These strategies were deemed more important than the curriculum of the school and the language of instruction. Mr. Sanchez made five trips to Mexico per week for his music contacts and practice, and his oldest son often went with him and finally joined the band. For the oldest son, Roberto, academic performance was heavily influenced by his incorporation into the band and his cross-border trips. The next youngest, Ricardo, did not take as many trips across the border. Ricardo had a close relationship with his mother, keeping her company and helping with the household chores. Staying at home allowed Ricardo to do homework in a relatively stable environment, in contrast to Roberto who did his homework in the car. However, Ricardo did eventually join his father's band as well. Both found girlfriends in Nogales, further complicating their academic performance. Later in Tapia's study all three of the oldest children graduated from high school.

The Mexican American families and students described can be considered somewhat characteristic of the United States–Mexican populations along the border. While it would be a mistake to stereotype every Mexican family based on this study, it is clear there are factors and influences in this specific demographic that are unique, and it would be a mistake not to consider them. Teachers need to place their students in an accurate context.

While there are many variations to these stories, they point out how a family's survival strategies and the structure and organization of each family's situation have direct and indirect influences on home-school connections and the students' academic success. The community's poor economic context also contributed to a less-than-ideal school-home situation. These perspectives present a more dynamic and heterogeneous view of students' learning than would a more stereotypical, uniform cultural model. There are some basic assumptions that can be made from Tapia's (2000) research:

- Compatibility between the language of instruction and interaction with students' and parents' home language facilitates learning. Students learn best in their native language; schools need to be aware of this, and they can help by communicating with parents in their native language. This is one important element that schools and teachers can mitigate. Schools can become more *user friendly* for language-minority parents.
- Change in a household's economic and survival strategies, in some contexts, are more important than language of instruction and school in general.
- There is an increasing influence of peers and family on student behavior as the students become older. Neighborhood social relationships sometimes limit high-level academic competence. There may be a limited number of high-achieving role models. Visits by minority community role models can help. One school sponsors minority trips to colleges and universities as a strategy to peak student interest and motivation beyond high school.

Of the 12 children in Tapia's (2000) study, most graduated from high school but none graduated from a college or university. These examples illustrate there are no easy solutions, and every family and student must be seen and dealt with as individuals. Stereotyping students in these communities will not serve a teacher well. In many cases schools compete with other elements within families and communities for a student's priorities and attention. Teachers may not have all the answers but empathy can go a long way to making a student's time in school a positive and stable experience for both parents and the student. Teachers should be ready to exhibit understanding, patience, and empathy.

Classroom Applications

In this era of high stakes test scores, the academic performance of minority children has been hotly debated in the media and in academic circles. It should come as no surprise that learning and academic performance are influenced by a range of factors and interactions between family and community economics, historical inertia, cultural norms, social norms, and linguistic background. All these factors interact with the student at home and in the community and come into the school and classroom.

Teachers need to consider adapting classroom instruction to these circumstances and try to accommodate the instructional program to meet the needs of the students and parents. Rigid, ultralinear programs will only frustrate students and parents. Frustration can mean that given a choice, family and personal concerns will win over school concerns, and the student may drop out.

Teachers need to make school important to students and their families, both from a student perspective and a parent perspective. Parents who have positive experiences at their children's school and who believe that school personnel want to work with them to help their children succeed in school are more likely to initiate contact with teachers and schools.

Precautions and Potential Pitfalls

Teachers often see students from these communities as problematic to their linear instructional agendas and programs. Rather than trying to fit students into a model of instruction that puts them at a disadvantage, teachers could use instructional models used by continuation schools and other similar programs that are designed to accommodate heterogeneous groups on different schedules and instructional pace.

Sources

Gutman, L. M., & McLoyd, V. C. (2000). Parents' management of their children's education within the home, at school, and in the community: An examination of African American families living in poverty. *The Urban Review, 32*(1), 1–24.

Tapia, J. (2000). Schooling and learning in U.S.-Mexican families: A case study of households. *The Urban Review, 32*(1), 25–44.

STRATEGY 56: Reflect on the complex issues surrounding school literature selection for bilingual and bicultural students.

What the Research Says

This study (Jones, 2004) focuses on the questions of which strategies are the most appropriate in determining how literature is selected and how reading preferences for bicultural and bilingual students are identified. It also reflects on the potential negative consequences for bicultural and bilingual students of not providing literature that reflects their situation. The prime focus of the study was to use data about students' reading choices to determine if they can find their own identities within the literature they read. Is their identity split between their two cultures? Should bilingual and bicultural be seen as separate cultures? In this study, Indian immigrants comprised the study group.

Jones then looked at minority publishing seen in Wales to explore the range of literature available. The goal was to identify positive steps teachers and schools could take in providing literature for bicultural and bilingual students that better connected to these students' backgrounds and intellectual needs.

Classroom Applications

When most students watch movies or read books, their own life experiences contribute to their enjoyment of the film or book. The more they share or identify with the characters or the situations presented, the more they like the book or movie. Conversely, the less affinity they share with the situations and characters, the harder time they have sharing empathy and enthusiasm. This is not always the case, but it helps if characters are dealing with situations they are familiar with in interesting and unique ways. Many people like to fantasize and place themselves in the stories and wonder what they would do.

Students living in a bilingual or bicultural environment may have a tough time finding books or movies that deal with their life experiences. Where are the heroes they need to help them shape their identities and give them their role models? Where are the books with gay and lesbian or bilingual and bicultural heroes? Chances are most school libraries and classrooms select books more in tune with the experiences of the staff and faculty or the majority culture at the school. Also, much of the curriculum today is mandated or selected based on potential tests down the road.

Material that fits the needs of local minority populations is often hard to find and screen for appropriateness. School demographics are very individual and localized. Today's schools are heterogeneous, and it can be very difficult to standardize inclusive films, videos, and literature for all schools. This doesn't mean that the need to address these concerns is not there. To meet the needs of these populations, each site must make the effort to dig for the materials to meet the needs of their own student populations.

Precautions and Potential Pitfalls

Be aware that taking responsibility for more appropriate materials for these populations may not be popular. Funding the needs of minority groups can be a very political activity. School budgets are always tight. Most minority groups and their parents don't have the "political presence" to exert much power over those who control the funding. It will take individual teachers or staff advocates promoting these types of concerns to make a difference. Very often these caring individuals will also need to do the searching and research to help select the materials and argue for the funding.

Source

Jones, S. (2004). Shaping identities: The reading of young bilinguals. *Literacy*, *38*(1), 40–50.

STRATEGY 57: *Carefully consider the use of cooperative groups with second language students.*

What the Research Says

In her 2004 study of 49 Chinese immigrant students, Xiaoping Liang determined that although many teachers used cooperative groups to build language skills in their second language learners, many students had conflicting feelings on the process of cooperative groups. Seventy-one percent of the students interviewed indicated that they both simultaneously liked and disliked cooperative groups. Liang identified three basic areas that created dilemmas for these students. Culturally, these students were aware of both collective social responsibility and the more modern trend of individual worth. These conflicting ideas extended into the second dilemma of socioeconomics as these students struggled with recent changes in the free-market system of Hong Kong extending into China. The students in this study were largely from affluent families and were very aware of the individual and competitive skills needed to succeed in a competitive global economy. Lastly, the educational paradox of working together as one value and grades and academic success being measured individually as another created internal conflict.

Classroom Applications

 Cooperative groups can be a positive experience for students who are learning a second language. It is vital, however, that teachers have specific plans in mind when using cooperative groupings. If the goal is to increase language use and acquisition, pairs may be a better starting point than a group of five students. Many teachers find that asking a question of the whole group, "What did you eat for dinner last night?" becomes a good starting point for a partner discussion. "Turn to your partner and share," also gives the teacher the opportunity to work with individual pairs and aids in authentic assessment. Additionally, teachers may want to extend pairings to other students, "Turn to your other partner and share what your first partner had for dinner."

When the goal includes content as well as language skills, cooperative groups may be an effective choice. To ensure their efficacy, teachers must concretely teach the cooperative skills needed before giving a content assignment to the group. Some teachers find that assigning specific group roles helps merge the individual accountability with the social responsibility of being part of a group. Giving students a card with a specific title and list of responsibilities can help facilitate the group process.

Other teachers may find that opening a dialogue with students about grading and the cooperative group process may contribute to some insight with a specific group of students. Older students who are able to voice their opinions and concerns are more likely to see the value in cooperative group activities.

Precautions and Possible Pitfalls

At first glance, this study might lead a teacher to abandon cooperative groups when working with second language learners. This would be a grave error as the benefits of language acquisition offered by cooperative groupings are significant. It is important that each teacher consider the skills and needs of the individual group of students before designing instruction for them.

Source

Liang, X. (2004). Cooperative learning as a sociocultural practice. *Canadian Modern Language Review, 60*(5), 637–669.

STRATEGY 58: *Explore the definition of literacy and the complexity of the term when applied to bilingual and bicultural students.*

What the Research Says

Jimenez (2003) argues for a broader look at how we interpret and define the term literacy. He states that the more formalized statements of literacy aren't "disinterested and detached musings" but rather active rhetorical efforts to legitimate the status quo and continue the privileges enjoyed by specific groups. His argument hints at a veiled form of institutional racism. Jimenez goes on to trace the interests of those doing the defining of literacy back to the author's defining identities, which draw from, reflect, or seem to be shaped by their ethnicity, race, class, gender, or other factors. He believes that current definitions of literacy do nothing to advance the academic achievement of marginalized groups, and these mainstream definitions of literacy will serve only to continue current institutionalized inequities. Jimenez's work is an anecdotal and literature-based exploration of attitudes toward literacy as they relate to bilingual and bicultural populations, specifically Latinos.

Jimenez (2003) identified some student groups as contributing to their own failure with a perspective that appropriate school-based forms of literacy need to be resisted as it is a form of domestication. Many other individuals have been defined socially and economically on the basis of their failure to acquire standard forms of English, Spanish, and other necessary levels of literacy, or, increasingly today, knowledge of technologies.

Many individuals and groups, Jimenez (2003) claims, have equally sophisticated but unrecognized abilities that should fall into an updated definition of literacy. He supports the idea that literacy researchers can contribute to the literacy discussion by identifying the unrecognized abilities students from diverse backgrounds bring to schools.

Classroom Applications

In today's educational environment of high stakes testing, teachers have less and less choice in what and sometimes how they teach. While Jimenez (2003) brings up some really good points, the reality of today's classrooms often means teaching a narrow band of mandated content, experiences, and related skills. Expanding the range of skills and knowledge that define literacy would seem to fly against today's political grain. However, individual teachers can begin to acknowledge and even celebrate diverse backgrounds, especially their students' unique literacy-based and communication-based cultural experiences. Acknowledging, highlighting, legitimizing, and expanding the range of multiple literacies and competencies within diverse populations can expand the range of options teachers have for supporting school-based literacy.

Researchers cited and described in the Jimenez (2003) study defined "out-of-school literacies" as a treasure trove of experiences and information with benefits for students and teachers. Out-of-school literacies exhibited by mainstream students are well known to teachers, and teachers can take advantage of these skills to promote school-based literacy. Mainstream students and teachers often share and see the same films, watch the same television shows, and generally share many cultural experiences that narrowly define literacy.

Some examples of out-of-school literacy skills illustrate a wider definition of literacy that teachers can build on. Bilingual and bicultural students are often depended on by their families for negotiating the demands of the English language and relating other cultural literacies. They often serve as translators for rental and lease agreements, income tax forms, and many other commercial transactions. They also aid in oral translations in stressful or fast-paced interactions. All these examples can be seen as alternative literacies. Many bilingual and bicultural students take these types of literacy seriously and see themselves as important contributors to the family.

These out-of-school literacies can serve to build bridges to improve literacy instruction. There are still questions about the relationship between these potential practices and those literacy practices commonly found in schools. Questions center on how this knowledge can be worked into curriculum or even if it should be worked into the curriculum.

Precautions and Potential Pitfalls

There is very little guidance and few rules for the teacher who wants to explore these concepts. In many states *literacy* is a very loaded political issue. Teachers need to be able to understand their local schools' and departments' political climates to know what they can do and what they can't. Every school is different in its curricular view and how it values diverse identities.

Source

Jimenez, R. T. (2003). Literacy and the Latino students in the United States: Some considerations, questions, and new directions. *Reading Research Quarterly, 38*, 122–130.

STRATEGY 59: *Actively address the diverse needs of English learners.*

What the Research Says

One in four California students is an English learner and 90 percent of teachers in California are monolingual English speakers. Researcher Balderrama (2001) demonstrates concerns that teacher certification programs may not be preparing teachers to adequately meet the needs of English learners or immigrant students. Balderrama is critical of the credentialing practices in California and cites that standards or examinations don't provide any opportunity for examination of the role of the teacher in the socialization and schooling of youth. They tend to "dance around" the importance of culturally responsive teaching while de-emphasizing the more qualitative and affective aspects of teaching.

An apparent conflict is the standards-based assessment of good teaching and the more humanized standards most adults use to reflect on how they remember good teachers. In the end it is the humanity that is emphasized in reflection, not teaching methods, techniques, or implementing standards.

Concluding, Balderrama's (2001) paper presents a context of teacher preparation with an emphasis on techniques and standards that tends to mis-prepare teachers in addressing the needs of an increasingly immigrant student population. The fear is that this mis-preparation will in turn mis-prepare the students academically.

Classroom Applications

Teacher education programs are ideologically based, and teachers need to understand the ideological underpinnings that tend to perpetuate social and economic subordination. They need to find a balance in their role as teachers from a technical perspective and sometimes, and more importantly, from a humanistic perspective.

When dealing with limited English proficiency (LEP) or English language learners, teachers will find that content and standards can be some of the least important things that they teach and they learn in their lives. Balderrama states

> In my attempts to raise the pedagogical consciousness of teachers, together we examine two elements of their teaching: 1) their students, within a historical context, and 2) the context of schooling and teaching. That is, students, particularly English-language learners, must be seen up close, not abstractly, so that understanding of their individual, academic and learning needs are humanized and thus fully understood. (Balderrama, 2001)

Teachers should include a critical understanding of a sociocultural context in their instruction and also use it to help guide their practices.

This type of teaching doesn't call on teachers to abandon all mandated guidelines, content standards, or expectations, only to find a larger and more relevant context for them within a larger picture of students' lives.

Precautions and Possible Pitfalls

Beginning teachers need to be careful to "take the pulse" of their workplace. Colleagues may be under great pressure to raise test scores and student academic achievement. It would be a mistake to ignore or neglect a teacher's responsibility to support school or department goals. However, teachers can create a more humanistic educational environment in which they and their students function. They will be expected to be accountable, but that doesn't mean they can't begin to explore a more humanistic approach to teaching and learning.

Sources

Valdez, E. O. (2001). Winning the battle, losing the war: Bilingual teachers and post-proposition 227. *The Urban Review, 33*(3), 237–253.

Balderrama, M. V. (2001). The (mis) preparation of teachers in the proposition 227 era: Humanizing teacher roles and their practice. *The Urban Review, 33*(3), 255–267.

STRATEGY 60: *Prepare for a cultural and linguistic mismatch between teachers and their students.*

What the Research Says

The majority of future teachers in the United States are white, monolingual, and female (Cushner, McClelland, & Safford, 1996). In contrast, the demographics for their students will increasingly be of a diverse culture and feature children of second-language learners (Hodgkinson, 1985; Pallas, Natriello, & McDill, 1989)

Because of this potential mismatch, future teachers will be called upon to teach in classrooms to a student clientele very different from their own cultural background. As a group, these new teachers will generally come from rural colleges and universities and will find their first assignments teaching in urban classrooms populated with second-language learners. They will bring a certain cultural, racial, linguistic, and economic background and expectations for urban life. These expectations will not likely be based on firsthand experiences. Here are the questions the researchers want teachers to consider:

- How does the experiential background affect how these teachers approach the urban experience?
- What expectations do the teachers have for urban students and community, and how does this affect their planning as they prepare materials for gifted and talented concurrently with curricular remediation?
- Do the teachers' management plans and strategies indicate they expect most of their students to behave and be internally motivated or to be difficult and unmotivated?
- Will the teachers feel comfortable with parent contacts community contacts, and home visits, or will they avoid communication and afterschool activities because they feel unsafe in the community?

Various studies (Terrill & Mark, 2000) point to future teachers exhibiting negative attitudes and perceptions toward urban schools and minority learners. They point out that most people tend to be culture-bound, and teachers with no experience in the backgrounds of their students are limited in their ability to interact effectively and professionally. They are not ready to shape cultural partnerships and teach in culturally diverse classrooms. These studies also found that teachers' personal experiences during childhood and adolescence were the major determinants of their cultural perspectives and most had little experience in diverse cultural settings.

Classroom Applications

 Teachers can look upon the potential problems presented by the research as their own or pass them off as a problem for the teacher education institutions. Teachers may think they will get that job in their first school of choice, but are they prepared to move on if they don't? What if a teacher's institution of higher education doesn't include a heavy dose of multicultural education throughout the curriculum? Will the teacher be prepared? The reality is teachers and their classmates will be competing for jobs in very diverse settings. The demographics point out that it is very likely a teacher will be working in a cultural demographic very different from his or her own. It is up to the individual teacher to squeeze every bit of help he or she can find within the program to become prepared. Teachers should seek out the professors who seem to be more in tune to multicultural themes and training. The new teacher will be better prepared to bridge potential cultural and linguistic gaps.

Next, consider service-learning opportunities in diverse settings. These experiences will increase levels of comfort and reduce anxiety. Teachers should be prepared to confront their cultural and linguistic assumptions, perceptions, and expectations. They will be able to help students with an expanded awareness and a more inclusive, tolerant, and larger knowledge base.

Finally, teachers should consider developing strategies to explore their own cultural, linguistic, and racial identities and biases. Teachers will find it is difficult to explore and appreciate the world views of others without a grasp of their own. As a teacher it is important to develop a knowledge base of the major paradigms and concepts of multicultural education, diverse cultures, ethnic, and social groups. Schools don't want educators who are afraid of their communities, expect the worst in the classroom, and rarely see their students as gifted and talented and being motivated.

Precautions and Possible Pitfalls

Teachers shouldn't assume their subject matter or content mastery is the most important factor in preparation for the classroom. Depending on the settings teachers find themselves in, management and people skills will make the job much easier. Multicultural educational settings require diverse teaching tools. One size doesn't fit all, and teachers will need to provide multiple learning pathways in the same class. Many students and classroom demographics will exhibit needs well beyond the curriculum content.

Sources

Cushner, K., McClelland, A., & Safford, P. (1996). *Human diversity in education: An integrative approach.* New York: McGraw-Hill.

Hodgkinson, H. (1985). *All one system: Demographics of education, kindergarten through graduate school* (ED 261 101). Washington, DC: Institute for Educational Leadership.

Pallas, A. M., Natriello, G., & McDill, E. L. (1989). The changing nature of the disadvantaged population: Current dimensions and future trends. *Educational Research, 18*(5), 16–22.

Terrill, M. M., & Mark, D. (2000). Preservice teachers' expectations for schools with children of color and second-language learners. *Journal of Teacher Education, 51*(2), 149.

STRATEGY 61: Select spell-checker programs that meet the needs of the specific student population.

What the Research Says

Spelling is one of those somewhat elusive and yet intrinsic skills that enable individuals to communicate clearly. It is a skill necessary for independence that may need to be mastered or compensated for within a written format and can be clearly understood by others to facilitate a successful transition into adult life. In fact, while many students with limited English skills are able to overcome deficits in reading and math, they often retain their spelling deficits well into their adult lives. The inability to spell correctly also inhibits and limits the effective use of spelling correction technologies. Helpful techniques such as dictionaries and personal word lists, which are commonly used to assist these students, can become relatively useless outside the school setting.

Researchers Coutinho, Karlan, and Montgomery (2001) and MacArthur, Graham, Haynes, and De La Paz (1996) examined the use of spell-checkers in the context of word processing. Spelling instruction must not only include acquisition skills and remedial instruction to overcome the spelling deficit, but also compensation skills and instruction that enable the student to write with accurate spelling. One popular compensation tool for writing is a word processing program. Students need to become competent users of these programs and their features (e.g., spell-checkers) that will enable them to compensate for spelling weaknesses. Spell-checkers provide target words for misspellings based on keyboarding and spelling rule application errors.

Unfortunately, for a spell checker to be useful for students with spelling deficits, it needs to provide the correct spelling for complex misspellings. According to the researchers, the spelling errors of students with learning disabilities are more complex than simple typos and rule application errors. In order for spell checkers to be a valuable tool for students with learning disabilities, the spell checker needs to provide the correct spelling for complex misspellings. The misspellings can often be classified as severe phonetic mismatches, having few of the phonetic characteristics of the target word. Often spelling choices appear less mature and may contain characteristics of younger children's errors.

With these factors in mind, researchers Coutinho et al. (2001) and MacArthur et al. (1996) surveyed a range of word processing programs to identify the programs that serve the students most successfully. To accomplish this, three questions relating to the use of spell-checkers by students with learning disabilities were addressed:

1. Do the various spell-checkers provide the target word for misspellings first in the replacement list?

2. Do the various spell-checkers generate the target word first in the replacement list equally across phonetic developmental level?

3. Do the various spell-checkers generate the target word first in the replacement list equally no matter what proportion of correct letter sequences (bigram ratio) the misspelling contains?

For this study, a search of software catalogs identified nine word processing packages that were designed for school use and included spell-checkers. Two of the nine word processing programs (Write This Way and Write Outloud) were designed specifically for students with disabilities. In addition, two word processing packages commonly used in college and university settings (WordPerfect 5.2 for Windows and Microsoft Word for DOS 6.0) and two word processing programs commonly sold with computer packages (Microsoft Works 4.0 and Claris Works 4.0) were included.

Classroom Applications

Because the range of students with spelling deficits vary widely, no single program is going to be the answer for everyone. As technology continues to develop at an amazing speed, teachers will need to continue to update their information regarding what works for their specific students in the context of the individual classroom. The best suggestion that comes out of this research is that when shopping for a computer program, spelling and grammar checkers are important considerations, and teachers should consider their usefulness with value for all student groups before making a final decision. Ease of use and range of ability levels are also important considerations in making a final evaluation.

Precautions and Potential Pitfalls

 Regardless of the software selected, it is essential that teachers take the time to become proficient in using the application, including becoming familiar with the various tools offered by the application to facilitate student use. It's always a good idea to contact colleagues who may be experienced with the software, and don't forget to access company help lines as needed.

Sources

Coutinho, M., Karlan, G., & Montgomery, D. (2001). The effectiveness of word processor spell checker programs to produce target words for misspellings generated by students with learning disabilities. *Journal of Special Education Technology, 16*(2), 27–41.

MacArthur, C. A., Graham, S., Haynes, J. A., & De La Paz, S. (1996). Spelling checkers and students with learning disabilities: Performance comparisons and impact on spelling. *Journal of Special Education, 30*, 35–57.

STRATEGY 62: *Consider portfolios to create an overview of student performance and growth.*

What the Research Says

 Influenced by Howard Gardner's multiple intelligence theory, the faculty of Crow Island School in Winnetka, Illinois, assessed and evaluated their 10-year journey and the evolution of their portfolio thinking. Overall, they found portfolios fulfilled the promises they felt portfolios held when they began. Reflections over this 10-year period explored the many teachings and learning experiences involving portfolio assessment. Key factors included timely and careful assessment. Their evaluation painted a clear picture of what portfolios are and what portfolios aren't. The staff defined and refined the roles of all stakeholders in the portfolio concept, and today they continue to gain a more in-depth view of their students as learners through the use of their full site-based, student-centered portfolio vision (Hebert, 1998).

Classroom Applications

Many industries require portfolios to augment or even serve as a visual resume of ability and performance. Many teachers find that student portfolios can offer the same kind of insight into student ability and performance. Portfolios also allow students to create and develop their own product for evaluation over time. This can be very helpful to document the growth of a student who is learning English. Portfolios can help demonstrate these students' progress, which is particularly important if the student is not meeting standards yet.

Portfolios can be designed to fit a variety of needs, and teachers can adjust their criteria over time to best capture student performance. In the beginning of a student's portfolio development, teachers would be wise to be flexible when deciding what goes into it. Teachers should consider allowing and helping students decide what goes into the *story* of their learning and growth. For some students, *telling* a long-term story is too abstract. Defining an audience for the work may contribute to a more concrete picture.

To attach meaning to each piece in a portfolio, ask students to write a short reason for its inclusion. This reflection tag contributes to the student's metacognitive growth and attaches further value and meaning to the individual content. This sort of language experience can strengthen emerging English literary skills. In addition, teachers need to determine how the portfolio will be evaluated. Many teachers find that a completion rubric works better than a traditional grading system, particularly if the included work pieces have been graded before being placed in the portfolio.

Precautions and Possible Pitfalls

 Portfolios can be a simple concept, but they can also turn into huge projects that require significant effort and time on the part of both teachers and students. Do not underestimate the learning curve involved. Expect some frustration during the implementation and transition to portfolio adoption and remember that just as students grow and develop over time, so can their portfolios.

Source

Hebert, E. (1998). Lessons learned about student portfolios. *Phi Delta Kappan,* 79(8), 583–585.

7

Working
With Parents

*It is time for parents to teach young people early on that in diversity
there is beauty and there is strength.*

Maya Angelou

**STRATEGY 63: *Develop strategies
to help parents help their children
succeed academically.***

What the Research Says

 Gutman and McLoyd (2000) used open-ended questioning
techniques to examine variations in parents' management
and organization of their students' education within the
home, at school, and in the community. The goal was to define parent
behaviors typical of successful students and contrast them with students
experiencing behavior and academic problems. Questionnaires focused on
how parents' encouragement of educational activities differed between
high-achieving and low-achieving students, and research explored how

these activities differed. This investigation also examined the frequency of parents' school involvement and the different reasons for involvement. Lastly, researchers explored the frequency of children's extracurricular and religious involvement inside and outside of school and how it was different for both groups. They also looked at why parents manage or fail to manage these activities.

Gutman and McLoyd (2000) found that parents of high achievers used more specific strategies to help their children with their schoolwork. They also had more supportive conversations with their children than parents of low achievers. Parents of high achievers not only were more involved, but also had different reasons for their involvement than parents of low achievers. In the community setting, parents of high achievers explicitly engaged their children in more activities to support their achievement.

The sample included information from 22 elementary schools and 10 middle schools with 42 percent African American students and with 84 percent of the total students involved in reduced-fee or a free lunch program. To select a subsample to identify high-achieving and low-achieving students, student grades were collected from school records, and groups were defined.

Classroom Applications

More parents of high achievers reported being involved in their children's school than parents of low achievers. The parents of high achievers were also involved in different ways, with more checks on progress as well as checks just to maintain contact. In contrast, parents of low achievers were involved with their students more for misbehavior or poor work. While both groups reported helping their children, parents of high achievers reported using more specific strategies to assist their children and participated more in supportive conversations with their children than parents of low achievers. Parents of high achievers frequently initiated contact with their children's school, whereas parents of low achievers rarely visited or made contact. High-achieving students were involved in more extracurricular and community activities than low achievers. Parents of high achievers engaged their students in community activities to support their academic goals. Parents of low achievers often discussed the personal barriers to the management of their children's activities and academic achievement. This involvement can have a significant impact on student achievement.

According to Clark (1983), students often perceive their parents' involvement in school as evidence of continued parental expectations for school success. Students reported that their parents accepted some responsibility for student performance at school.

Teachers, schools, and communities can support lower-income families with low-achieving students in many ways. Schools and teachers can help parents help their children with their schoolwork by organizing practical help programs that give parents the necessary skills to prepare their children for specific classroom lessons. For example, when assigning long-term projects, teachers might include suggested activities and assignments in a "parent section," and suggest sources of information or other resources including lists of related TV programs that support curriculum. Teacher Web sites, while not available to all parents, also help by providing class and school information.

Teachers can also promote positive interactions with parents through recognition of their involvement as a valuable resource for their children's achievement. To encourage parental involvement, teachers can stress positive developments over problem areas. Positive paper take-home messages and phone calls can help connect parents positively to school.

Teachers may want to offer suggestions for involvement in programs that don't rely on parental participation or permission for student involvement. Promoting the school's extracurricular programs and activities, not just to students, but also to parents, can increase student participation. The effort should be made to make these programs accessible to parents with hectic lives.

Precautions and Potential Pitfalls

Some of the suggested strategies will make it easier for parents to become engaged in positive ways with their children's academic experiences. However, there will be parents who still don't respond. Children of these parents need to be included to prevent them from feeling left out or somehow less worthy than other students. Too much touting of parental involvement can be hurtful for these students.

Sources

Clark, R. M. (1983). *Family life and school achievement: Why poor black children succeed or fail*. Chicago: University of Chicago Press.

Gutman, L. M., & McLoyd, V. C. (2000). Parents' management of their children's education within the home, at school, and in the community: An examination of African American families living in poverty. *The Urban Review*, 32(1), 1–24.

STRATEGY 64: Include parents from marginalized groups by making them feel welcomed.

What the Research Says

 Abrams and Gibbs (2002) examined Lareau's (1987, 1989; Lareau & Horvat, 1999) work on social class differences and family/parent-school relationships, involvement, and intervention in their children's schools. Then they overlaid the major concepts from the research across a community and the restructuring of a diverse elementary school in Northern California. Lareau's work reveals that parents who are familiar with the language and style of educational discourses are more inclined to participate in their children's schooling. Lack of functional literacy in these discourses can create barriers for many diverse parent categories based on racial, ethnic, economic status, language, or social class differences.

Accepting the tenets of Lareau's finding, Abrams and Gibbs followed the efforts of the New Washington School, a K–5 public elementary school located in urban Northern California, to restructure parent-school relationships with more carefully devised inclusive parental involvement strategies. Their study focused on a parental demographic with a median income of $21,554; 26 percent were two-parent households, and 50 percent of the single-parent households with children younger than 18 years fell below the federal poverty line. The student body included 35 percent Latino, 35 percent African American, 20 percent white and 10 percent Asian students. The questions they tried to answer were

- Can a change in school policies alter traditional patterns of parent-school relationships?
- What are the mechanisms that facilitate these changes in the patterns; where do these patterns of exclusion exist?
- Where are they broken down?

They found that the potential for social change was often obstructed by the mechanisms of social and cultural reproduction infused in individual power relationships and agendas between social class and ethnic and cultural groups. Conflicts and tension became the outcome of diverse perspectives and meeting styles. Different agendas inhibited compromise.

It's clear from this study that bringing traditionally marginalized individuals and groups together comes with issues for consideration. Many individuals were not familiar with the protocols of school discourse and the subtle and not-so-subtle micropolitics of special interest perspectives in school settings. In this case, while avenues for participation were constructed, the school did not set up clear directives about parental roles, and the school felt more solid intervention and training might have helped avoid some of the conflict and tension over power distribution.

Bringing parents together in restructuring situations highlighted the contested nature of schools and their programs in a diverse pluralistic society. In many cases, larger social relationships were acted out in the forum of the perceived role of public education within the contested needs of societies. Schools needed strategies to mediate power relationships in environments of competing needs and concerns about children's education.

Classroom Applications

Many parents see the school and the classroom from the singular perspective of their student's unique needs and goals. If the school is involved in a program of parental inclusion, teachers may be dealing with parents who have no experience in school discourse. Teachers are called upon to not only respond to parent concerns and needs but also to educate the parents in the workings of the classroom and the school. Parents may not have had a positive experience with school as students or may have different educational values and expectations.

It is often difficult for teachers to see schools and classrooms from alternative societal or cultural perspectives. However, in an urban setting, developing these strategies for positive participation is a must for creating an environment of mutual respect with diverse parents.

Communication is often the key to building successful parent-teacher relationships. While written notes may be a common starting point, if parents are functionally illiterate in English, oral communication through phone calls or conferences will be more effective. Many teachers find that student-led conferences early in the year can facilitate good communication and a positive relationship between parents and teachers.

Precautions and Possible Pitfalls

Parents come to the playing field of educational interaction from their relative social locations, and these positions often define their styles of interactions with the school and also each other. By helping to make marginalized groups and individuals feel included and welcomed, teachers may alienate and create some resentment among parents from more traditionally privileged social or cultural groups. They might not always agree with new parental leadership programs and policy changes, or they may see them as a threat to their power base. Real change is a challenge, and threatening traditional power relationships comes with consequences. Think about strategies to help prepare all stakeholders for the coming changes ahead of time.

Sources

Abrams, A. S., & Gibbs, J. T. (2002). Disrupting the logic of home-school relationships: Parent involvement strategies and practices of inclusion and exclusion. *Urban Education, 37*(3), 384–407.

Lareau, A. (1987). Social class differences in family-school relationships. *Sociology of Education, 60,* 73–85.

Lareau, A. (1989). *Home advantage: Social class and parental intervention in elementary education.* New York: Falmer.

Lareau, A., & Horvat, E. M. (1999). Moments of social inclusion and exclusion: Race, class, and cultural capital in family-school relationships. *Sociology of Education, 72,* 37–53.

STRATEGY 65: *Involve minority and culturally diverse parents as resources in the classroom.*

What the Research Says

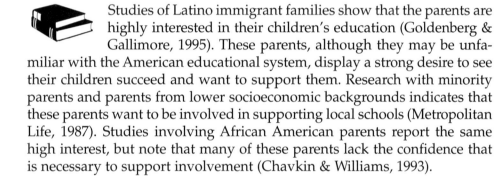

Studies of Latino immigrant families show that the parents are highly interested in their children's education (Goldenberg & Gallimore, 1995). These parents, although they may be unfamiliar with the American educational system, display a strong desire to see their children succeed and want to support them. Research with minority parents and parents from lower socioeconomic backgrounds indicates that these parents want to be involved in supporting local schools (Metropolitan Life, 1987). Studies involving African American parents report the same high interest, but note that many of these parents lack the confidence that is necessary to support involvement (Chavkin & Williams, 1993).

Classroom Applications

Some teachers may feel uncomfortable in using parents of minority and culturally diverse students as resources in the classroom. This reluctance often stems from concern about language difficulties and cultural differences. And yet, because of our changing population, all teachers should expect a diverse population of students. The challenges facing teachers in these diverse settings require social understanding that goes beyond the aspects of culture often approached in teacher education classes. Teachers need to give thought to the proper handling of major holidays, religious customs, dress, and food. Many teachers express a need for a more comprehensive kind of insight into the social ideals, values, and behavioral standards of the cultures of their students. Individual cultures have different approaches to child-rearing and schooling, and having a working understanding of these approaches helps teachers include parents more effectively.

For example, many teachers focus on critical thinking and Socratic questioning techniques. These emphasize a students' active class verbal participation. If a student is from a cultural background that stresses quiet respect in school, he or she may need to be taught how to become a more active participant in class discussions. Teachers can help this process by communicating with parents about active participation. Teachers can also provide participation opportunities, such as journal writing or small-group discussions to help build communication skills.

Teachers may want to pre-plan small group activities to include students from different cultural backgrounds. These students can then work together to build language skills as well as content comprehension.

Many teachers find that allowing students to work in small groups to preview their homework assignments helps improve homework completion. Students can discuss possible strategies for problems to ensure that all students have a basic understanding of the assignment. This also helps students whose parents may not be able to read the assignment in English, as well as those whose parents may not have the time or skills to assist at home.

Parent volunteers can be used in a variety of ways. Guest speakers on various topics (culturally related or not) can enhance instruction and provide variety. Some teachers find that having parents assist in managing small group or learning center activities can also facilitate learning.

Teachers need to make the effort to learn about the various cultures represented by their students. Parents are an excellent source of information as are the students themselves.

Precautions and Possible Pitfalls

Parents of immigrant and culturally diverse students can be an untapped resource in today's classrooms. Care should be taken to keep parents informed through communication (either written or verbal) in the parents' native language, if their English is not proficient. The teacher must also be aware that just because he or she sends home information in the parents' native language, the parents may still not be able to read or write in that language. It is not uncommon to find parents who have had no formal education before immigrating to the United States. The more information teachers can have about students, their family and their cultural identity, the more teachers can best work with parents in supporting students' learning.

Sources

Chavkin, N. F., & Williams, D. L. (1993). Minority parents and the elementary school: Attitudes and practices. In N. F. Chavkin (Ed.), *Families and schools in a pluralistic society* (pp. 73–83). New York: State University of New York Press.

Goldenberg, C., & Gallimore, R. (1995). Immigrant Latino parents' values and beliefs about their children's education: Continuities and discontinuities across cultures and generations. In P. Pintrich, & M. Maehr (Eds.), *Advances in motivation and achievement: Culture, ethnicity, and motivation* (Vol. 9, pp. 183–228). Greenwich, CT: *JAI* Press.

Metropolitan Life. (1987). *Study of minority parent involvement in schools.* New York: Author.

Trumbull, E., Greenfield, P. M., Rothstein-Fisch, C., & Quiroz, B. (in press). *Bridging cultures between home and school: A guide for teachers.* Mahwah, NJ: Lawrence Erlbaum.

STRATEGY 66: Consider the positive and negative effects homework has on students and their families.

What the Research Says

Buell and Kralovec (2000) cite homework as a great discriminator as children, once leaving school, encounter a range of parental support; challenging home environments; after-school jobs, sports, and other obligations; and a mix of resources that are available to some and not to others. Clearly, opportunities are not equal. Tired parents are held captive by the demands of their children's school, unable to develop their own priorities for family life.

Buell and Kralovec (2000) provide examples of communities that have tried to formalize homework policy as the communities tried to balance the demands of homework with extracurricular activities and the need for family time. They also point out the aspects of inequity inherent in the fact that many students lack the resources at home to compete on equal footing with those peers who have computers, Internet access, highly educated parents, and unlimited funds and other resources for homework requirements. They also point out that homework persists despite the lack of any solid evidence that it achieves its much-touted gains. Homework is one of our most entrenched institutional practices yet one of the least investigated.

The big questions their research and discourse explores are: "With single-parent households becoming more common or with both parents working, is it reasonable to accept the homework concept, as it is now practiced, as useful and valid considering the trade-offs families need to make?" "How does homework contribute to family dynamics in negative or positive ways?" "Does it unnecessarily stifle other important opportunities or create an uneven or unequal playing field for some students?"

Classroom Applications

Teachers need to carefully consider the intended purpose for specific homework assignments. Some tasks offer students the opportunity to practice their skills, some offer remediation, and some invite students to go above and beyond concepts covered in class. Teachers need to evaluate the time commitment required to complete the given assignment, and one of the best ways to accurately estimate that time frame is to actually do the assignment. While it may seem advantageous to foster students' understanding of geography by having them create a relief map, the actual complexity of the task and time and materials involved may outweigh the academic benefits. In addition, families with limited means may find the project simply beyond their financial scope.

Teachers need to consider the individual makeup of their students with regard to culture and socioeconomic status. Teachers need to be considerate of religious observances and plan homework assignments and test dates accordingly. Consider the inequalities that may exist within the range of students in your classes regarding their ability to complete homework assignments.

Some teachers have found it effective to sponsor homework "clubs" that meet before school, at lunch, or after school to help level the playing field for students who lack support or other resources at home. Often teachers will work together to provide these services so each teacher is not called upon to work extended hours everyday.

Precautions and Possible Pitfalls

Traditionally, homework has been seen as a solution to educational problems rather than a cause. Although it seems obvious that the more time students spend in academic endeavors the better their skills and performance will be, that time commitment needs to be balanced with time spent with family, friends, and extracurricular activities.

Source

Buell, J., & Kralovec, E. (2000). *The end of homework: How homework disrupts families, overburdens children, and limits learning*. Boston: Beacon.

8

Establishing and Sustaining Your Professional Identity

I know the price of success: dedication, hard work, and an unremitting devotion to the things you want to see happen.

Frank Lloyd Wright

 STRATEGY 67: Actively seek opportunities to expand personal experiences in multicultural settings.

What the Research Says

 Personal background is recognized as an important element in the development and formation of multicultural perspectives in teachers. These previous experiences and backgrounds influence what is taught, the teacher's interpretations of classroom situations, student behaviors, and many instructional decisions. The main background elements of this perspective are race, gender, and social membership; prior experience with diversity; and support of ideologies of individualism (Smith, 2000).

Two related studies looked at the following issues:

- How do the background experiences of preservice teachers influence inclusion of a multicultural perspective in teaching?
- How do preservice teachers' background experiences influence the effectiveness of a teacher education program in achieving multicultural education?
- How could a multicultural immersion program alter their perspectives?

One study examined two preservice teachers, one with limited multicultural experiences and background and another with multicultural experiences in her background. Both were white. One was mainly isolated in her socioeconomic and cultural upbringing, and the other was immersed in and forced to fit into and adapt to other cultures in other countries. Both taught history in schools of roughly the same size. One teacher's school was slightly more diverse. Overall, the data, from observation, teacher reflection, and student responses, suggest noticeable differences in the two teachers' effectiveness as multicultural teachers. Background experiences and specifically three factors—the teacher's race, gender, and social class; prior experiences with diversity; and support for ideologies of individualism—appear to offer a partial explanation for these differences. While the two subjects seemed to be at opposite and extreme ends of the multicultural spectrum, the researchers felt there were valid concerns both teachers could bring to education programs with regard to how background experiences influence them: sensitivity and cultural congruence; knowledge of students' background; awareness of learning styles; recognition of racism, classism, and sexism; and high school students' perceptions of teachers' teaching.

This case study provides tentative support for the explanatory power of teacher background in a teacher's ability to respond to multicultural pedagogy. The results of this study found a connection between multicultural background and a teacher's ability to deal with multicultural settings. However, the researchers did recommend further studies using larger sample sizes and a wider range of research questions.

Another study (Wiest, 1998) examined how a very short-term immersion in a multicultural setting affected a group of student teachers or teachers within a teacher preparation program. Three classes of 86 students in their fifth year of a five-year education program were asked to immerse themselves in an unfamiliar multicultural experience of their choice and respond with project write-ups. Settings ranged from African Americans in church to gay bars and Quaker meetings. Students had to take the initiative in their self-growth by arranging their cultural immersion experience themselves.

Most students were reported as being displeased with the assignment and expressed discomfort and anxiety during the project. After project completion, however, they overwhelmingly endorsed it as valuable and memorable and stated it was the most important course assignment. However, the experience did have a neutral effect on a few, and some made little effort to fully engage and immerse themselves. Others expressed a feeling of guilt about infiltrating a group without explaining why they were there. Others were resistant to the situation they entered, and this compromised the effectiveness of the experience.

Judging from the feedback, the researcher felt that the project had a meaningful effect on the students but made no claims about the lasting or cumulative effect of multicultural activities assigned in addition to this project.

Classroom Applications

 The research speaks to experience as the best teacher in preparation for a multicultural placement. Classroom discussions and activities can only go so far in their contribution to a teacher's range of multicultural insight and tactics. There is a good chance a teacher's first job may occur in a social, cultural, or ethnic environment he or she is not familiar with. These studies point out the need for teachers to fill in the multicultural gaps in their training.

Getting a teaching job is only the beginning. All new teachers will be working toward keeping the job. More important, teachers strive to personally feel effective and in control of any situation they are asked to tackle. The more a teacher experiences and the more understanding and knowledge he or she brings to the job, the more comfortable that teacher will feel.

Some suggestions for how to gain that experience include volunteering for placement in unfamiliar settings, scouting out the communities ahead of time, reflecting on personal fears and limits, finding support from community groups and colleagues, researching and reading the professional literature, and seeking professional inservices and workshops.

Precautions and Possible Pitfalls

Preparation for a multicultural setting is very individualized, and each teacher needs to be honest with himself or herself and very proactive. Individuals, based on their unique needs and goals, may have to go well beyond their current knowledge to fill in holes in their preparation. Teachers shouldn't underestimate the challenges a multicultural classroom of students, their parents, and the community can present.

Sources

Smith, R. W. (2000). The influence of teacher background on the inclusion of multicultural education: A case study of two contrasts. *The Urban Review*, 32(2), 155–176.

Wiest, L. R. (1998). Using immersion experiences to shake up preservice teacher views about cultural differences. *Journal of Teacher Education*, 49(5), 358–365.

 STRATEGY 68: Internalize that cultural experience and perspective are different for each individual.

What the Research Says

The recruitment and retention of minority students in teacher education programs have received increasing attention as concern for retention of minority teachers in urban schools grows. There is widespread support for the idea that teachers of color are more likely to understand and embrace the culture of their minority students and therefore be fundamentally better equipped to provide culturally sensitive instruction and pedagogy for minority students. Frank's (2003) study focused on listening to the voices of African American education majors enrolled in teacher education programs at predominately white universities in the United States. The goal was to try to understand how their experiences might affect their perceptions of teaching and behaviors as future teachers. Their experiences offer an opportunity to appreciate the challenges they face in predominately white education programs.

The basic premise of Frank's (2003) research was to develop greater understanding of minority teaching students' experiences and how these experiences might affect their perceptions of a particular educational setting. With this information, the profession can better support and retain minority teaching candidates.

This was a qualitative study designed to collect data from informants in educational settings that would help outsiders construct meaning. Long-term group discussions helped the researcher understand how African Americans' experiences in predominately white schools might affect their perceptions of teaching. The focus of this data gathering was on how the participants perceived their prior education and their experiences at university. In addition, these discussions revealed where they saw themselves teaching and what type of teacher they might be expected to become. In this case, participants were actively engaged in "making sense" of the educational setting, defining the meaning intended by others, and inventing and reforming new personal meaning.

The researcher facilitated a total of 13 focus-group meetings once per week over a five-month period. Ten female African American students participated. They ranged in age from 18 to 30 years old. Most had limited exposure to predominately white educational settings. All were less than 12 months from completing their requirements for a state teaching certificate. The 13 focus group meetings provided participants' perspectives on a variety of issues. Data gathering centered on why participants made the decision to attend a white university, their relationships to experiences at the university, and their relationship to their culture and identity construction.

Classroom Applications

 First and foremost, minority educators, particularly African American educators, face unique challenges in predominately white colleges, universities, and other educational settings. All teachers should reflect on how their personal perspective and experiences affect the way they interpret events and other teachers' and students' behavior. This is particularly true of new teachers coming from backgrounds that create mismatches between their cultural experiences and their students' cultural experiences.

Teaching style is something that develops over time and is enhanced by exploration, experience, and trial and error. The greater the mismatch between any individual educator and the students he or she teaches, the less shared experiences they have and the more effort it takes to create a positive interaction. It is important to formulate a personal and unique teaching style to become effective in many situations and with many student backgrounds and communities. For teachers with a white background, it is not sufficient to read about the perspective of people who have been oppressed.

The effort should be made to begin to view society and education as a collective whole rather than the "haves" versus the "have nots" consumers of public education. It is important that all teachers explore their background, perceptions, and how they could relate to their current educational setting. Greater empathy and understanding of the students and their community are the goals.

Precautions and Potential Pitfalls

As this research points out, the greater the mismatch, the further teachers are pushed out of their comfort zones and the more help they need to see their students in an accurate context. Teachers need to move slowly and respectfully as they explore their students' cultural experiences and context. These efforts to communicate that respect should emphasize confidentiality and a student's ability to choose not to share as is appropriate.

Source

Frank, A. M. (2003). If they come, we should listen: African American education majors' perceptions of a predominantly white university experience. *Teaching and Teacher Education, 19,* 697–717.

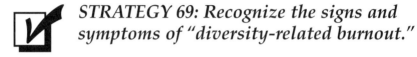

STRATEGY 69: *Recognize the signs and symptoms of "diversity-related burnout."*

What the Research Says

Tatar and Horenczyk (2003) introduced the concept of "diversity-related burnout," which is described as the ways in which a teacher's personal and professional peace of mind or well-being is adversely affected by the day-to-day interaction with a culturally diverse or a highly heterogeneous student demographic. This study was able to distinguish this specific diversity-related burnout phenomenon from the more traditional versions of teacher burnout.

The study had two main objectives. First, to examine whether diversity-related burnout is empirically distinguishable from general teacher burnout; and second, to explore the extent to which diversity-related burnout is predicted by variables related to cultural heterogeneity of the school and to the teacher's background (job role, years of teaching experience, and level of the class taught).

This study looked at data from 280 teachers working in 30 different Israeli schools that reported having immigrant students in their classrooms. Fifteen schools in the study were primary schools and 15 were secondary schools. Teaching experience ranged from 1 to 37 years in the classroom. Schools were sampled from various parts of the country, and the majority of immigrants (almost 20 percent) came from the former Soviet Union. The classrooms represented various compositions of socio-economic backgrounds.

Tatar and Horenczyk (2003) found ample background evidence to support the idea that teachers lack the information, skills, and motivation necessary to cope with the challenges of the multicultural setting they were experiencing. In addition, it was also noted that the teachers' preservice experiences generally provided little interaction with or knowledge of students with backgrounds different from their own.

This study found that diversity-related burnout could be distinguished from the more traditional notion of teacher burnout. It was also revealed in the study that burnout could be predicted by variables related to the teacher's background, the degree of the school's cultural heterogeneity, and the school's response to multicultural issues.

The research supported the idea that the highest level of diversity-related burnout was found among teachers classified as "assimilationists" and in schools perceived to also be assimilationist schools. Proactive and reactive strategies for preventing and reducing diversity-related burnout were discussed.

Burnout can be described as one type of chronic response to the accumulation of stress from long-term negative impact of work stresses. The general factors (Maslach & Leiter, 1997) that contribute are

- Emotional exhaustion, a general feeling of being overly stimulated or overextended by contact with students
- Depersonalization or feeling a less-than warm response toward students as recipients of a service
- A feeling of low personal accomplishment or a decline in feeling of competence and satisfaction with one's teaching
- A feeling that efforts to help others have been ineffective, the associated tasks seem mundane and unchallenging, and the personal rewards and payoffs have not been forthcoming

As a consequence of these feelings, burned-out teachers generally provide less valuable information and less praise to students, show less acceptance of their students' ideas and thoughts, and more frequently avoid interaction with students. They also tend to affect and lower staff morale overall. Often schools are forced to work around teachers who are burned out.

Classroom Applications

Diversity-related burnout factors add to the Maslach and Leiter (1997) list. First, when dealing with diverse students, additional challenges affect a teacher's instructional style and subject matter content. The behavior of students of diverse classrooms is likely to be seen as different and more challenging, and communication with their parents may seem more problematic.

Tatar and Horenczyk (2003) found that attempting to assimilate diverse students contributes to burnout. On the surface, assimilation may seem more uniform and less time-consuming, but it does not reduce stress. Teachers need to recognize the issues presented by a diverse student population rather than ignoring that diverse range of needs. Adopting a differentiated instructional model that embraces the range of cultural and educational needs of students is more likely to meet with success. Research found that pluralistic multicultural educators in pluralistic school settings demonstrated the lowest degree of diversity-related burnout.

Cultural trends today generally favor pluralistic multicultural approaches to diverse classrooms. However, assimilation philosophies are still held by some and not just in the dominant culture. There are individuals in all cultures that favor assimilation for their students. However, the findings of Tatar and Horenczyk's (2003) study call for interventions targeted at promoting pluralistic attitudes toward classroom instruction. They also noted that resistance to diversity creates a barrier to the benefits of teacher training and the ability of a teacher to work effectively in diverse classrooms.

Hopefully, once individuals are made aware of the additional diversity-related factors that are identified and contribute to burnout, teachers and administrators can act in proactive ways to mitigate them. If diversity-related burnout is reflected in a teacher's behavior and perceived by others, changes can be made to enable the teacher to better cope with the elements of burnout. Finally, diverse classroom strategies can and should become a louder voice in the conversations of all educators.

Precautions and Potential Pitfalls

Recognizing the symptoms of traditional burnout or diversity-related burnout is only a start. Personal reflection on a teacher's own cultural identity and philosophy must be explored, together with the identification of the elements of diversity-related burnout in that setting. Institutional responses may not always provide proactive or reactive solutions to the burnout symptoms.

Many times, individual teachers will need to act on their own to evaluate diverse classroom situations with new and fresh perspectives. Teachers working in culturally diverse settings can then survey and adopt useful strategies to reduce the stresses and tensions involved in teaching. This may include developing a more effective support system or creating and adjusting personal expectations for what can and cannot be done. The most important thing a teacher can do is begin to develop a sense of importance regarding multiculturalism and how it affects the classroom.

Source

Maslach, C., & Leiter, M. P. (1997). *The truth about burnout: How organizations cause personal stress and what to do about it.* San Francisco: Jossey-Bass.

Tatar, M., & Horenczyk, G. (2003). Diversity-related burnout among teachers. *Teaching and Teacher Education, 19,* 397–408.

STRATEGY 70: Become knowledgeable about adolescent culture.

What the Research Says

 It is no secret that some of the most difficult challenges facing beginning teachers are classroom management, physical and emotional isolation, and difficulty adapting to the needs and abilities of their students.

Brock and Grady (1997) concluded, "Teaching is one of the few careers in which the least experienced members face the greatest challenges and responsibilities." Many beginning teachers come prepared with book knowledge and theory, but the reality of controlling a classroom of 35 students is a whole other story. This reality usually hits after the first few weeks of school when the honeymoon period is over for the students and they have figured out what they can and can't get away with in a particular class.

In many teacher preparation, induction, and mentoring programs across the nation, these issues are being addressed with concrete solutions and qualified mentors. Connecting with exemplary veteran teachers who have experience and rapport with adolescents can also be a big help. New teachers at the secondary level report their teacher colleagues having a positive influence in helping them understand the challenges of adolescents. Conversely, elementary teachers felt their principals were extremely helpful in providing support and encouragement.

Classroom Applications

 No longer can we tolerate a "sink or swim" attitude. In California, the BTSA (Beginning Teacher Support and Assessment) program focuses on beginning teachers learning as much as possible about the students in their classrooms. The languages spoken at home, previous student test scores, the community in which these students live, and cultural and socioeconomic knowledge all help novice teachers understand and adapt to the needs of the students they teach. Teachers should check literature, music, and clothing trends, and spend time looking over popular magazines and checking on students' favorite films and television shows. Most important, they should take time to talk to and listen to the students themselves.

Precautions and Possible Pitfalls

With the social climate today and students coming to class with a myriad of challenges and concerns, it is more important than ever for teachers to be aware of the problems and challenges of adolescent culture. What may seem trivial to an adult can be monumental to an adolescent. Many students would rather be considered "bad" in front of their peers than "stupid." Yet many times a novice teacher will put students in the position of acting out because they don't know the answer to a question. It is important not to judge students based on what other teachers say. All students deserve teachers who have not made up their minds on what the student is capable of in the classroom. Teachers should be careful of becoming too much of a "buddy" or "friend" and not retaining adult status, modeling adult ideas and behavior. The more teachers can invest in understanding their students, where they are coming from, and what is important to them, the more successful they can be in implementing classroom management procedures.

Sources

Brock, B. L., & Grady, M. L. (1997). *From first-year to first-rate: Principals guiding beginning teachers*. Thousand Oaks, CA: Corwin.

Lortie, D. C. (1975). *Schoolteacher: A sociological study*. Chicago: University of Chicago Press.

STRATEGY 71: *Do not underestimate the preparation necessary for placement in urban multicultural settings.*

What the Research Says

This study (Barry & Lechner, 1995) examined a group of preservice teachers' awareness and attitudes about various aspects of multicultural teaching and learning. Seventy-three of the students enrolled in undergraduate teaching methods classes at a large university in the southeastern United States participated in the study. The majority of the subjects were white females. Surveys and questionnaires were the primary sources of data.

Results indicated that these education majors were aware of many issues related to multicultural education and anticipated a diverse classroom experience in their future. Most were undecided and had little confidence (60.3 percent) as to just how well their teacher preparation had developed their abilities to teach children from cultural and religious backgrounds other than their own. This included communication with their families. However, 49 percent felt confidence in their ability to locate and evaluate culturally diverse materials. The major recommendations and conclusions focused on education programs and coursework discussing potential changes and alteration to teacher training curriculum and pedagogy.

Classroom Applications

 Often people look to colleges and universities for expert opinions on a wide range of topics. Academics make a living creating new knowledge and act as repositories of the most current thinking on many of the major issues of today. However, teachers should not necessarily find security in their ability to train for a multicultural experience. Research suggests that there is a wide range of competency within teacher education programs nationwide.

Most teachers are culture-bound and have little experience looking at life through the eyes of other ethnic and religious cultures and socioeconomic levels. The most common suggestions for teacher candidates centers on individuals volunteering for service and/or finding a local knowledgeable, nonjudgmental mentor in school districts a teacher thinks he or she might apply to. Both suggestions can be arranged in any number of ways both formally and informally.

The teacher can ask school personnel in the district for suggestions on how best to become prepared. Another suggestion focused on selectively picking faculty members in a teacher education program who offer the most practical and realistic help in preparing teachers for placement in ethnic-sensitive settings.

If teachers plan to apply to multicultural urban schools, they can take a proactive role in seeking out the right kind of help before becoming disillusioned because of lack of preparation or naiveté.

Precautions and Possible Pitfalls

There are not many pitfalls in becoming more proactive in these matters. There is no secret that ill-prepared teachers become very disillusioned about teaching and their career choice. Teaching is hard enough without underestimating the potential rigors a teacher might face in unfamiliar settings.

Source

Barry, N. H., & Lechner, J. V. (1995). Preservice teachers' attitudes and awareness of multicultural teaching and learning. *Teaching and Teacher Education, 11*(2), 149–161.

Index

**CORWIN
PRESS**

The Corwin Press logo—a raven striding across an open book—represents the union of courage and learning. Corwin Press is committed to improving education for all learners by publishing books and other professional development resources for those serving the field of PreK–12 education. By providing practical, hands-on materials, Corwin Press continues to carry out the promise of its motto: **"Helping Educators Do Their Work Better."**